ARTIST DEVELOPMENT

A distinctive guide to the music industry's lost art

BY EUGENE FOLEY

Edited By:
HEATHER ROZEK & MATT CHEPLIC

Design By:
JANI DUNCAN-SMITH, IT GIRL DESIGN

COPYRIGHT © 2005
FOLEY ENTERTAINMENT, INC.

ISBN 0-9770715-0-2

LCCN 2005905639

Additional copies of this book are available by mail.
Please send a money order for $15.00 (USD) per book to:
Foley Entertainment, Inc.
PO Box 358
Greendell, N.J. 07839 USA

Printed in the U.S.A. by
Morris Publishing
3212 East Highway 30
Kearney, NE 68847
1-800-650-7888

Eugene Foley

ACKNOWLEDGEMENTS

I would like to thank my wife, Heather, and our children, Lauren and Joseph, for their love and support.

Thanks also go to my parents, Eugene and Camille Foley, for always encouraging my academic and creative pursuits.

Thank you to John and Frances LaGreca for their continued enthusiasm and help.

My sincere appreciation is also extended to Matt Cheplic & Heather Rozek for their help with editing this book and Jani Duncan-Smith for her outstanding graphic design and creative vision.

I would also like to thank the following people for their friendship, kindness and professionalism. Each of these amazing men and women continue to make meaningful contributions to the music and entertainment industries on a daily basis. I respect them all and sincerely applaud their efforts: Sylvia Rhone, Ahmet Ertegun, Strauss Zelnick, Craig Kallman, Don Grierson, Derek Sivers, Alex Steininger, Darren Hamedl, Brian Mahoney, Steve Parry, John Billings, Robert Haber, Ritch Esra, John Seymour, Scott Rush, Andy Karp, Greg Johnson, Jason Jordan, Mark Mazzetti, Mark St. John, Stan Pietruska, Ted Weis, Steve Brown, Jim Nelson, Andy Wubbenhorst, Mitch Santell, Paul Reed Smith, Jim Cullen, Winn Krozack, John Kasyc, Hal Selzer, Blake Althen, Paula Bellenoit, Steve Waite, Christine Yandell, John Harris, Vikki Walls and everyone at Disc Makers, CD Baby and PRS Guitars.

Eugene Foley is the Founder & President of **Foley Entertainment, Inc.**, a music industry consulting firm and licensed Entertainment Agency Foley Entertainment, Inc. represents artists, labels, managers, executives, producers, engineers, mixers, songwriters, publishers, session musicians, recording studios and other industry participants.

The firm provides a variety of professional services, including career guidance & direction, marketing, promotion, advertising, publicity, media buying, shopping campaigns, and artist development programs. Foley is a licensed Agent, and is recognized as an accomplished expert in music industry consulting, intellectual property and artist development. He is one of the music industry's most sought-after, respected and trusted consultants.

Foley lectures extensively at prestigious music conferences, conventions, seminars, colleges, universities, law schools, festivals and special events across the country. Armed with a law degree (with an emphasis on Entertainment Law & Intellectual Property) and gifted with a golden ear, Foley has successfully blended his academic accomplishments with his outstanding creative skills.

Realizing the importance of remaining on the cutting edge of one's profession, Foley continued to expand his knowledge by taking numerous continuing education courses at two prestigious Ivy League institutions, Harvard University and Cornell University. His advanced studies at those schools concentrated on executive leadership, executive decision making, strategic thinking, marketing and Internet marketing, among others.

His interest and fascination with politics, government and scholarly research also led Foley to pursue and earn a Ph.D. in Political Science. It was a personal goal, unrelated to business, that Foley nonetheless worked hard to achieve in his spare time. Affectionately known as "Dr. Gene" by industry friends and clients, Foley is a first-class music executive who has an unparalleled understanding of the creative process and the talented people behind that amazing process. Clients have come from all fifty states and nearly twenty foreign countries since Foley Entertainment was launched in 1989.

Foley and/or his clients, have contributed to projects involving the following major record companies, in various capacities, at some point in their respective careers: Atlantic, Columbia, A&M, Epic, Arista, CBS, Universal, MCA, EMI, RCA, Sony, Lava, Interscope, Hollywood, Polygram, Elektra, Capitol, Chrysalis, Mercury, Polydor, Geffen, Warner Bros., Windham Hill, Narada Jazz, Verve & Island/Def Jam, among many others.

Clients have earned nearly 40 Gold & Platinum Records & three GRAMMY® Awards for their overall career accomplishments. Foley is a frequent contributor to music related features on MTV, VH1, Fox, NBC, CBS, ABC, PBS and to numerous magazines and publications including Forbes, Variety, The New York Times, Fast Forward & Millimeter.

In 1996, Foley was the co-author of the acclaimed book; "How To Make It In Music In 6 Months... and 18 Years." Foley's partner on that project is former Columbia Records recording artist, Steve Parry.

Foley is licensed with the New Jersey Office of the Attorney General, Division of Consumer Affairs, Office of Consumer Protection/Regulated Business Section. He is an active/voting member of N.A.R.A.S. (The Grammy Awards) and a member of the Better Business Bureau. Foley is also an associate member of the Fraternal Order of Police. He is involved in activities, fund drives and public awareness campaigns for The National Neurofibromatosis Foundation and The Special Olympics.

In his spare time, Foley enjoys tennis and playing his collection of Paul Reed Smith guitars. He is also a sports car enthusiast and avid wine collector. Foley lives in New Jersey with his wife and their two children.

MISSION STATEMENT
Eugene Foley & Foley Entertainment, Inc.

The mission of Eugene Foley and Foley Entertainment is to provide outstanding professional consulting services and distinguished instruction to our Clients, in a wide range of music industry disciplines, including, but not limited to; artist development, marketing, promotion, publicity, advertising, songwriting, composing, arranging, intellectual property, publishing, touring, distribution, producing and merchandising, along with advanced career guidance and direction.

We strive to cultivate the highest possible level of Client achievement through passionate, inspirational and innovative contributions to every project that we take part in.

We carefully prepare our Clients to successfully meet the challenges and opportunities that they encounter in the ever-evolving music industry. We offer a genuine resource that nurtures and encourages all musical genres, comprised of an outstanding and truly global client base.

Our efforts assist not only musicians, but songwriters, label executives, producers, engineers, managers, publishers, teachers, session players and numerous others industry participants.

We are committed to enriching and enhancing the lives of musicians, songwriters and the entire music community with educational seminars, lectures, workshops, clinics, mentoring and scholarly activities. Our company helps Clients increase their knowledge and understanding, at a level that is appropriate to each individual's interests and needs.

We will continue to deliver music industry exposure, inspiration and wisdom to Clients, while endowing the music industry with the talent and vision our company is so justly known for.

EUGENE FOLEY
Founder & President

TABLE OF CONTENTS

INTRODUCTION

Artist Development, A Distinctive Guide To The Music Industry's Lost Art, is geared towards educating struggling artists, musicians, songwriters, managers and owners of independent labels about one of the most important topics in this business, Artist Development. Sadly, this is a crucial topic that is clearly being ignored by many record companies these days.

Countless people have taken up an instrument at one time or another, but only a handful will actually persevere to the point of attaining meaningful and lasting success. Several months ago, I decided to write a book that focused on the important subject of Artist Development, while covering a handful of other topics that I felt were also beneficial to up and coming songwriters, musicians, managers and other industry participants.

I knew that entire books are written about each of the topics covered in this one, so that was not my goal. I wasn't looking to wax poetic for 400 pages about music publishing or some other subject. I wanted to write a book that was easy to read, practical, helpful and straight to the point.

Have you noticed the decline in the quality and depth of records lately? How many of today's new artists do you think will still be making marketable and relevant music thirty years from now? There was once a time when labels would spot an artist that they believed in and slowly bring that project along until they reached superstar status.

After signing, the A&R representative would closely work with the artist in song selection, song arrangement, producer and studio selection and even help find outside songwriters if needed. Record company executives would then brainstorm with the artist to develop an image and a long-term marketing and promotion plan. Note the phrase, "long term."

In the past, the artist/label relationship was entered into with the expectation that it would be a long and mutually beneficial arrangement. Once the debut record was released, grassroots marketing and constant touring were often the staple of the artist's early years.

A scenario that was prevalent "back in the day" — involving an artist that wound up being successful, would be like the following example. An artist would be signed and then head to the studio to cut a record. Upon the release of the album, marketing, promotion and touring campaigns would be launched. The first record might sell 100,000 copies as the artist slowly secured the respect of the fans, the print media, radio and retail. Then after repeating the entire process, the sophomore record would perhaps sell 250,000 units. By the third release, the artist would really explode and record sales would surpass 1,000,000 copies. From there, this artist could probably put out several more well received records, continue to tour and remain relevant and respected in the eyes of the fans and the media for years to come.

Thanks to the developmental efforts and patience of the label, the artist in this made up scenario had a chance to properly develop in all areas of their career and was poised for a lengthy run at or near the top of the charts.

A typical scenario in today's music industry would be like the following example. An artist has a great song or two, built an impressive level of buzz on college radio and the support of the press in their market. They sold 10,000 or more CDs on their own and live shows are drawing 500 each night. The artist is polished and professional in every way conceivable. They get signed, cut a record and a video and get put out on tour.

Once the record company feels that the album has reached its peak in sales and it appears that the second or third single is not being embraced by radio – then the artist is dropped soon thereafter and everyone moves on. It's not quite that fast, but I'm sure you get the picture.

I can't place all of the blame with the labels. They are under enormous pressure to release great music that sells a large amount of albums. If they invest a certain amount of time and money into an artist and things just aren't taking off, they have every right to drop the project and cut their losses right there, before incurring any more debt. They are in business to earn money and if something is not working, the rules often dictate that it's time to cut bait and look for the next artist.

But years ago, this business-like mentality was not so prevalent. Creative executives gave creative artists the time and resources to build something slowly from the ground up. This mentality is not seen as often these days. Often, artistry has a way of getting lost in today's system.

Of course, some artists in the past have been dropped quickly and some artists of today have been given the time and resources to develop. But speaking in general terms, if an artist in today's climate wants to have a long and successful career, they better come to the table developed, polished and ready to go. If they think a major label will wave some magic wand and take them from the garage to the arena's stage overnight, they are sadly mistaken. Yet some artists continue to believe that's a route they can take to the top!

Today's artist must find other ways to develop each element of their career. It may be a manager, an agent, a consultant, a lawyer, a producer or a small independent label. It must be someone who has the expertise, knowledge, contacts and patience to take you from Point A to Point B. If you can successfully navigate that opportunity over time, then you may be ready to approach the larger record companies.

In today's world, I look at the major record companies as a wonderful source for promotion, marketing, tour support, financial support and retail distribution. They are great at that, without a doubt. If you think the majors will hold your hand as you try to turn good songs into great ones – forget it. If you think they will try to introduce you to college radio and the print media for the first time, dream on my friend. And they won't be sniffing around your door if your live show is weak. Please do your homework and don't allow yourself to be fueled by unrealistic expectations.

You better put together a great team and then invest your time and money into developing the project. If you can make yourself very well known and successful in a large market, you'll have a chance to get recognized by the majors and top indies and possibly be promoted to the big leagues. Later in this book, I will discuss forty markets across the country that I feel have a great original music scene.

Here are a few things you can start working on:

- Assemble your team.

- Get your songs, CDs, press kit, live show and plan in place.

- Choose the market or markets that you want to target in your campaign.

- Become wildly successful on the radio stations and in the newspapers in those markets.

- Sell a ton of CDs and merchandise.

- Pack the venues every single time you play.

- Try to secure some national press.

- Keep track of your success and continually update your press kit.

If you can pull this off on a large scale, the majors will find out and may even start reaching out to you, in an effort to see what the commotion is all about. It would then be a good time to start formally shopping the project, to make sure all of the labels that are appropriate for your project receive a package.

If your goal is to remain unsigned forever and put out records on your own, then you may choose to follow several of the above pointers – but fine tune the plan accordingly and begin to expand into other markets when warranted. But remember this, all ye people who buck the notion of signing with an established label.... It costs a ton of money to record, manufacture, promote, market and distribute original music nationally. Add in video and touring costs along with retail promotion campaigns and the number is astronomical.

If you have the cash, great. If not – it will be nearly impossible to sell hundreds of thousands of records without the support of a large record company. Their expertise, clout, financial resources and retail distribution can never be underestimated. Never. To date, I haven't met any truly unsigned acts that had the financial ability to support sustained national promotion, marketing, publicity, advertising and touring campaigns. (Let alone having top retail distribution in place and the funds to properly handle retail promotion opportunities.) Independent record companies are also an excellent opportunity to nurture and advance your career. Some of the smaller labels still have the time and patience to develop artists that they believe in. I'll discuss major and indie labels in more detail later in the book.

You really have three choices:

- Remain as a truly independent artist for a period of time, or forever.

- Sign with an established independent label.

- Sign with a major label.

My advice comes down to this… Develop your project the best you can with the help of your team of professionals. Try to make yourself the most well known and successful artist in a large market. When the time is right, present yourself to the top record companies and music publishers. It sounds so simple, doesn't it? Well we all know that it's not an easy road.

But if you come to the table with the right package, you will at least be in the running for a successful career. If you just aimlessly meander along on your own path, without taking the most prudent steps, then your career will never reach its potential.

14

With more and more record companies not investing time into artist development, someone has to teach the finer nuances of this forgotten and invaluable art. In athletics, skilled players can learn their sport and improve with hands-on training in college and later in the minor leagues, before graduating up to the "majors."

In the music industry, most people do not have access to that opportunity. Generally, record companies are looking for artists that are polished, developed and prepared in every way. They can then fire up the publicity, promotion and marketing machine and let the artist roar up the charts.

The larger labels often avoid the time and financial risk of taking a talented young artist and investing the proper resources to bring them along slowly. It's a better "business decision" to find an artist that is already seasoned and with a strong buzz in place. It cuts down the risk of taking someone to the top all the way from square one.

But what about the countless people who need development and are not fortunate enough to have a caring and knowledgeable manager, label or mentor in their corner? Are they ultimately destined for failure? I don't think that's fair. What? Only the chosen few will have the chance to hone their skills and have a real shot at making it? I have been working with musicians and songwriters every day for well over fifteen years in a variety of capacities. I see the same handful of mistakes when people send in their CD and press kit for review and feedback. Every week I speak to people who are spinning their wheels in frustration, while they continue to make the same amateur errors over and over.

So obviously, not everyone is taking the time to read the 400 page textbooks. Time, effort and money are being wasted by too many people. None of us are getting any younger and time is of the essence in our industry. I felt that it was time for me to release a reader-friendly book that musicians, songwriters, managers and new independent label owners would make the time to read. A book that would help them and inform them on many important issues, all relating to developing an artist. I chose topics that I see people having the most confusion about in my everyday experiences.

I believe that the length of this book makes it readable for even the busiest of people. If some of the information in this book educates you, enlightens you, entertains you, clears up a misunderstanding that you had about the business or encourages you to research even deeper on certain topics, then I will have accomplished my goal. I truly hope that my experiences can help you learn and evolve so you reach your full potential.

A large portion of the packages I receive are weak, flawed and need a serious makeover. And it's not just me. I speak with executives at labels, radio stations and magazines every day who are experiencing the same thing. If after a quick perusal, you feel some of the topics in this book are "basic" or "for beginners only" or "common sense" - then think again, my friend.

I am a huge fan of statistics. I love collecting data and then analyzing it to learn and improve. By looking at information and trends, it's clear to see that regardless of how many books, seminars and conferences are out there, a large number of people are still missing the boat. Some folks are missing it by a mile!

So for years now, I've been keeping track of the number of packages that arrive at my office. Then after reviewing the CDs and press kits, the submissions are divided into three categories that I've come up with for my own internal tracking. The first is Pass, the second is Development and the third is Pro.

PASS
About 10% of the packages I review fall into the "Pass" category. These are packages featuring CDs and supplemental materials that are extremely poor in quality and appearance. In most cases, it's people who cannot sing or play their instruments. I gladly and politely provide feedback to these people, but I'm not a miracle worker, people! PASS! Drive through please.... Next!

I'll review anyone's CD and happily give them advice and some pointers. I actually enjoy doing that. But if someone is formally invited to become a client of Foley Entertainment, it means I believe in them completely and without reservation. It also means that I like them as a person too. Someone can be an amazing talent, but if I don't feel a positive chemistry or I don't feel our vision is on the same page, I must respectfully decline that person's request to join my client roster. Sadly, the road must end after the initial feedback is given with certain people. I prefer not to waste people's time and I don't want anyone wasting mine either.

DEVELOPMENT

The second of my three categories, and the one the majority of people fall into, is called "Development." About 75% of the artists are in this group. These are people who are clearly talented, professional and working hard to advance their respective careers. But, unfortunately, they are coming up a bit short. With some direction, development and guidance, they can quickly be on their way to the next level.

Usually their press kit needs some refining or more content has to be added. The other common problem for those in Category #2 is song arrangement weaknesses. For whatever reason, they did not structure their songs in a manner that is acceptable, at that given time, in the radio and A&R worlds. Forty-second intros will not endear you to pop A&R executives!

These are issues that can be remedied quite easily after a phone consultation with yours truly and another trip to the recording studio to polish up a few things. Once the songs are in order, it's time to develop a plan and then start executing it.

Most people appreciate my honesty and guidance. You're better off learning the truth and working towards improving, rather than heading down the street to hire another company who will accept your money, even if they don't believe in your project. Some people will take you on as a client as long as you have a CD, a check and a pulse. I'm not one of those folks. My apologies, but you must be great to work with me. Or… good, with the potential to be great and the sincere willingness to work hard to reach that esteemed level. If you're lazy and unfocused, please don't waste the time of any ethical industry professional. There are too many other people out there who are talented, hungry and willing to do whatever it takes to make it.

One of my greatest professional joys is giving someone advice and direction and then listening to their new CD a few months later. Seeing the development and evolution of their music and supplemental materials is a wonderful thing for me. When someone goes from a "7" to a "10" in a few months, I'm very proud of them. Most talented people simply need a little guidance and some moral support. With that, they can go a long way. Once the music is where it needs to be, I'm happy to begin brainstorming with the artist about marketing, promotion, publicity and all of those exciting topics!

PRO

About 15% of the packages that arrive fall into the third category, simply known as "Pro." These are artists that have great songs, a professional press kit fill of meaningful accomplishments and a super live show. Thanks to the wonders of DVD, I get to see acts from around the world right from the comfort of my comfy leather chair! Get the popcorn kids!

Artists in this category already have significant success at college radio and with the press. Most have sold between 1,500 and 10,000 CDs and a good amount of merchandise. If an artist in this category is interested in shopping for a record deal, then my answer would be yes. It's time to roll!

I've noticed that many of the artists that are in my "Pro" category usually had some help along the way, either from a manager, lawyer or producer. But I do get packages from people who had no professional help, yet still put a polished and impressive presentation on my desk. But this is very rare.

People always hear about "overnight success stories." Granted, this may occur once in a blue moon, but the overwhelming majority of stars have achieved their goals by dedicating their entire lives to music. An enormous amount of effort is necessary for an artist to reach the top, and an even greater amount is necessary if they want to stay there for any length of time. Talent alone does not guarantee that an artist will be able to make a success out of their career.

It's not very realistic to think that you're going to be discovered performing in your neighborhood bar by a record company executive. It could happen, but it's quite unlikely. In order to succeed, an artist must integrate the proper combination of innate talent, knowledge of the business, planning, perseverance, tireless effort and good fortune. You have to get things really cooking on your own, before any heavyweight record company executive will give you the time of day.

I have always been a believer in designing and implementing realistic game plans. I am more of a realist, compared to some people who live in a fantasy world. Many times, I use a baseball-related analogy to describe my philosophy. I'd much rather hit a bunch of singles and steadily score runs, than swing for homeruns on every pitch and strike out 99% of the time.

I prefer to deal with the realities of our industry, rather than making decisions based upon misinformation, lack of knowledge or fantasy. I decided to touch base about the topics that I see the most people having a hard time grasping for whatever reason. Music remains one of the preferred forms of entertainment in the world. The vast majority of consumers feel that, compared to television, books, magazines and movies, recorded music exceeds the expectations that compelled them to purchase the product in the first place. Music is one of the few mediums that can be enjoyed for years to come, compared to a movie or magazine that is watched or read once and ultimately cast aside. As competition increases for the consumer's entertainment dollar, music is proving to be the mainstay for the global population.

I've had the pleasure of working in many areas of the music business throughout the years. My experiences have included being a musician, a songwriter, a session player, a guitar instructor, an artist manager, a recording studio owner, an author, an agent and a senior consultant to established record companies. I've been an executive producer and creative consultant on many records too.

I've contributed to campaigns involving every level of

19

recording artist, from small town unsigned acts, to projects with some of the biggest names in the music business. I've done it all – and have learned a great deal over the years. Hopefully I can pass along some of that experience and insight to you.

This book represents the opinions and professional philosophy of the author. The content of this book is for information purposes only. It is not a substitute for legal or other professional advice. Always consult with your attorney, accountant, or other professional for guidance and direction about your particular career needs. I applaud you for making an effort to learn more about the music business and in developing your career. Good luck and may all of your dreams come true!

Eugene Foley
August 1, 2005 – New Jersey

THE SONGS

Your dreams are filled with lights, limos, and champagne. You can picture yourself giving an acceptance speech at an awards show while friends and neighbors say, "We remember little Johnny when he was just the boy next door."

When you wake up in the morning, you're ready to leave the garage behind and change the world with your music. But remember this... literally millions of other people have the same goal as you around the world. You need every advantage that you can find to make it in the highly competitive and uncompromising music industry. To effectively compete, you must learn all that you can so your entire presentation is at its best.

For starters, you must begin to prepare your demo and press kit. This is how you will introduce yourself to the professionals who run the music industry. Before you even begin preparing a press kit, you should examine the role of the demo in your presentation. The demo is the backbone of the press kit. The songs on the demo are what separate the good acts from the great acts. Pure and simple, hit songs are the most important element in securing a recording contract. Never forget that!

You may well be very talented. You may even be in the most popular unsigned group in your town. But in the industry's eyes, you are probably still unknown and unproven. To prove yourself worthy of their time and backing, you must write songs as strong as (or stronger than) the songs on the radio. Don't waste time and money recording and promoting "average" songs. You must take the time to write and rewrite your songs over and over. Polish the material until you truly feel that they have reached their full potential.

Compare your song arrangements to that of successful songs within your genre. For example, if your music is similar in style to U2, how well do your songs stack up against theirs? I don't necessarily mean in terms of recording quality, but in other areas, such as arrangement and structure.

If your songs do not measure up, you'd better begin the rewriting process. There is no shame in rewriting your songs. There is, however, shame in rushing through the songwriting process and not giving your songs the justice that they deserve. Remember that writing songs is not a race. You are judged by quality, not quantity. You are better off with three great songs, rather than twenty weak ones.

And don't tell me or any other music industry professional that your songs are hits "as is" because "your friends told you so." While it's great that you have their support, they are probably not in a position to sign you to a major label. And if they are.... then congratulations on your good fortune!

Each song needs a memorable hook, or chorus. In order for a song to leave a lasting impression, it must be catchy enough to remain in the listener's mind after hearing it only one or two times. The chorus must capture the listener and keep them interested in the song both lyrically and melodically. Do not force rhymes or squeeze in words simply to fit the melody. Make sure that the lyrics say something in a way that no one has said it before in a song. If the song feels contrived or phony, you better start editing!

Try to write about topics that the average listener can relate to and understand. Make sure the theme or story line is clear and the images are vivid. No one wants to be a mind reader or a police detective just to figure out what you're talking about. Save the hidden meaning stuff for your poetry project. You may also consider avoiding controversial subjects that could perhaps alienate a large part of your potential listening audience.

As you arrange the song, try to keep the introduction to around 10 seconds if possible. You should also work hard to reach the chorus by 40 to 42 seconds. If your chorus is coming in at 43 seconds or more, begin editing now!

If you are a rap songwriter, you should try to reach the chorus around the 55 second mark. The verses are traditionally longer in rap than in pop, rock and R&B music, therefore your arrangements will be slightly different.

Try to keep the song's total time to be approximately 3:15 to 3:45. This is especially important if you are hoping to secure radio airplay for your material. Most radio stations will not play a song that is over four minutes long.

The style of popular music song arrangement that I recommend is as follows:

- Introduction

- Verse One

- Chorus

- Verse Two

- Chorus

- Bridge/Solo

- Chorus (2x)

This is, of course, only one way of arranging a commercial pop song, but it's a style that is quite common. If you write and perform in other, more niche styles of music, it's important for you to analyze successful songs in your genre and arrange the material accordingly. Since the majority of my clients are striving for commercial success at radio, support from the media and acceptance from record company A&R executives, I prefer very commercial arrangements in songs.

As you compose and arrange the verses, the chorus and the bridge, make sure the music and lyrics are strong and memorable. Make sure the dynamics are there, so the average listener can tell when the verse ends and the chorus begins. Try to avoid using clichés in your lyrics or rhymes that are very common, such as "heart" and "apart." Come up with something fresh and new.

You should also keep in mind what key a song is written in as you compose new material. If you're writing for a specific singer, make sure that the song is written in a key that they can sing in comfortably. A singer's range is much more limited than that of a guitar or piano. Often, the lead vocal track becomes the nucleus of the song. Try to accommodate your singer so his or her talents can be maximized.

The next important area of songwriting is the tempo. The tempo creates a special feel and pace for the song. Be sure that the words aren't being squeezed in just to keep up with the music. There has to be a smooth flow between the lyrics and the music. Also, do not make the mistake of forcing rhymes just so you can complete a verse. Take the time to find the correct way to express what you are trying to convey to the listener.

Successful songwriting also involves creating your own style. An artist or group's songs should break new ground. You must create and develop a unique sound that fits within a specific musical genre, yet allows you to retain the integrity of your vision. This is not easy, but through years of learning their craft and constantly rewriting, successful songwriters have been able to achieve that elusive goal.

It has been my experience that a hit song is one that sounds great even with minimal production, such as only a vocal track and a piano. Heavy production will not transform a mediocre song into a hit. Trust me on that one! The proper combination of lyrics, melody and vocals are necessary to produce a hit. Without all of those elements, a song has no hope for real commercial success. Technology can sometimes make a song with a poor foundation more interesting, but only the right blend of the three basics will give a song real soul and passion.

A useful and easy way to evaluate and improve your songs is by recording rehearsals. It is a great way to check your song's arrangement, melody, and overall presentation before booking expensive studio time. When you listen to a recorded version several times, it is easier to focus on specific areas, without the distraction of actually playing your instrument. You can rewind a tape or scan a CD as often as you need in order to get the feel of a particular section. It also allows you to envision the presentation that you will be making to the eventual listener.

A serious mistake that some artists make on their demo is when they try to appeal to a dramatically broad audience. Many acts have crossover potential, which is the ability to attract fans from several styles of music. In moderation, that can be wonderful and quite helpful in building a large fan base. But it's not what a demo should be highlighting, especially if this lack of "genre focus" is taken to the extreme.

Whether you are a solo artist or a music group, you do not want a demo with one rock song, one country song, and one rap song. You need to show industry professionals that you have a specific sound and style. They will not be impressed with your so-called versatility. It will only look like a lack of vision and direction.

Most artists do not like having their music categorized, but it is something that happens. Record companies and promotion people have to target a certain market when they are promoting a new act. Regardless if it's rock, rap, pop, dance, country, or jazz, it will have a genre classification. Classifying an artist's music allows record company marketing executives to better plan an act's promotional campaign. This would include which radio stations to approach for airplay, and which music publications to contact for articles and reviews concerning the act.

Sending a rock CD to a rap station is a waste. So pick a style and keep your focus there. If you're a rock group and you happen to have a ballad that eventually crosses over to the pop radio charts, that's wonderful! But in those early days – pick one genre and do it great. I can't believe how many CDs I receive that feature songs that are clearly two different genres. I'm not talking about songs that tastefully blend rock and rap, or jazz with blues. I'm referring to the CDs where one song is in the punk genre and the very next tune sounds like techno. Please master one thing and stick with it.

The A&R executives (Artists and Repertoire - record company talent scouts) are looking for an intangible quality in your songs that will separate your CD from the hundreds of others on their desks at any given time. Most labels either specialize in one genre of music or have separate A&R reps for each style that they work with. Since their job is to find artists in a specific style, they are taught to automatically weed out any talent that does not conform to the boundaries of the music genre in which they are working with.

When it comes to personal style, every songwriter has influences that have contributed to their sound. The difference between a superstar and a glorified cover band is the ability of the artist to find the right balance between early influences and creating their own unique sound.

In many industries, innovators and pioneers are the people who not only make the most significant contributions to their industry, but are the most celebrated and remembered. In the music business, this is especially true. Being a flavor of the day artist may work for a little while, but it's not the foundation to build a long and successful career. Record companies invest a great deal of money in a new artist. They want their acts to stay at the top, so they can both recoup their investment and make a handsome profit.

Usually, a record company will not sign an artist unless they feel that they have the potential for a lengthy career. I don't think too many label executives actively pursue an artist that is clearly destined to be a one hit wonder. But as we all know, some artists have one hit and then dramatically drop off the charts, much to the dismay of the record company.

Take your time as you begin to get songs together for your

demo. It does not make sense for artists to pay the high cost of studio time until their songs are completely ready to be professionally recorded. Polishing material through multiple revisions and rehearsals gets expensive when the clock is ticking at one hundred dollars per hour or more.

With home recording equipment being reasonably priced these days, you should consider purchasing some basic recording gear and a good microphone. This way, you can take your time writing, rewriting, editing, and polishing your songs. Everyone must have their respective parts well rehearsed before you enter a professional recording studio. You don't want to spend three hundred dollars to watch your guitarist waste studio time trying to compose and cut a solo for one of your songs. Be sure to do your homework where it belongs... at home!

Obviously, a large, commercial studio would be a wonderful way to record a demo. The sound quality is indisputably superior, and the extra tracks also allow for a more unique and developed product. However, I have heard many great demos that came out of a 16-Track home recording facility over the years.

Once your songs are written, edited and rehearsed, you are probably ready to begin recording. If you are looking to release a full length CD with ten to twelve songs, it tells me your goal is to sell as many units as possible. Giving the consumer that many songs adds value for them.

If your goal is to have a nice product to not only sell at shows, but to utilize as your calling card to the music industry, then I feel four or five songs would be perfect. That should equate to about fifteen to eighteen minutes of music. The CD could be sold to fans for five dollars. It can also be used as you approach venues, labels, publishers, radio stations, managers, booking agents, the press and other industry pros.

Due to the large number of demos that music industry professionals receive on a daily basis, they can only afford to spend a few minutes listening to each submission. If someone is impressed with your work, they can always request to hear more material.

I always felt that a demo should start off with an up-tempo song, then a mid-tempo. I like to see a ballad in the third slot and close the disc with another up-tempo number or two. This will demonstrate versatility within your given musical genre. Music industry professionals are impressed by an artist's ability to successfully write and perform the full range of their particular style and genre.

Note the line..... "of their particular style." Therefore, if you are the singer in a rock group and you happen to be a great jazz sax player in your spare time, don't bother showing off that skill on your rock CD if it's not appropriate. Always make sure your best song is placed first on the disc. (Because if the first one doesn't catch their ear, they may not even listen to tracks two, three or four.)

When making copies of the demo to send out to industry executives, use a compact disc. Try not to send cassettes or vinyl if at all possible. If vinyl is still popular in your genre, try to send the industry executive a CD and the vinyl, or ask them which they prefer.

Your graphic design should neatly incorporate the artist's name, address, phone number, e-mail address, Web site, song titles, and copyright information. If you forget to label every-thing properly and a record company or manager likes your songs, they will not be able to contact you.

To this day, I receive several CDs per month with no cover letter and no contact information on the CD itself. I can't believe that people continue to make that mistake! Then some people have the nerve to call me and ask why I haven't responded with feedback. I'm not a private eye, therefore I cannot spend an hour trying to track someone down. It's a safe bet that other industry pros will feel the same way. So make sure everything is labeled.

Also, if you're burning the CD yourself, make sure you check each one before-mailing it out. At least once a week I receive a blank CD, due to some technical error by whoever was burning the disc, and they sent it without realizing their mistake. Have you ever heard about the importance of first impressions?

I recommend that you work with an experienced, knowledgeable and reputable company such as Disc Makers to design and manufacture your CDs. I have worked with them since 1989 and they have never disappointed me or a client. Their quality, value and customer service is second to none. The number is 800.468.9353. In all honesty, I can't see why an artist or label would go anywhere else for such an important aspect of their career. Remember the name... Repeat after me.... Disc Makers..... See, that was easy!

The last thing that I want to mention about songwriting is "rejection." Anyone in this business will hear "NO" far more often than they will ever hear "YES" from industry executives. This is not a business for people with thin skin. It's not easy putting hard work, heart and soul into a song, only to have it rejected by twenty A&R executives a month later. Sure, it hurts and it stings and it causes every emotion from anger to disappointment. But put the shoe on the other foot for a moment. A rep at a major label or top publisher is reviewing literally thousands of songs and packages per year. He or she may only have the budget or authority to sign a small handful of those submissions. To preserve their own job, they better be correct enough of the time while deciding what to sign and when to pass.

Remember the importance of patience. Successful executives are very busy people. They receive hundreds of packages and hundreds of calls each week. If it takes someone a month or longer to respond to your follow up, deal with it. Be polite and be glad that they at least listened to your music. Try to learn from any feedback that they give you and express your appreciation for their time and comments. Perhaps if you call a few months later with a new package, they'll agree to take another listen. If you're rude, pushy or a pest, you will probably burn that bridge forever.

Try to become familiar with the material of other great songwriters and performers. It's not only an educational experience, but one of inspiration as you evolve as a writer and artist.

Here's a list of records, in no particular order, that I feel demonstrate outstanding lyrics, music, arrangement and production. I tried to include artists in a variety of popular genres. You may already own a few of the records on this list. These are some of my favorites. I'm sure I could have added two-hundred more if time and space permitted.

- Everything by the Beatles

- Led Zeppelin – "Led Zeppelin IV"

- AC/DC – "Back In Black"

- Boston – "Boston"

- Pink Floyd – "Dark Side of the Moon"

- Everything by Bruce Springsteen

- Garth Brooks – "No Fences"

- Bob Marley & the Wailers – "Legend"

- Eric Clapton – "Unplugged"

- Prince – "Purple Rain"

- Def Leppard – "Hysteria"

- Phil Collins – "No Jacket Required"

- Bon Jovi – "Slippery When Wet"

- Kenny G – "Breathless"

- Madonna – "Like A Virgin"

- Van Halen – "Van Halen"

- REM – "Out of Time"

- U2 – "The Joshua Tree"

- Lionel Richie – "Can't Slow Down"

- Guns 'N Roses – "Appetite for Destruction"

- Nirvana – "Nevermind"

- Alanis Morissette – "Jagged Little Pill"

- Green Day – "Dookie"

- Metallica – "Metallica"

- Pearl Jam – "Ten"

- Jewel – "Pieces of You"

- Everything by Eminem

- Creed – "Human Clay"

PRESS KITS

This is yet another area that most people take for granted, but many are still not doing it correctly. I would say that at least 70% of the packages sent to me do not contain all of the elements that it should. That is an alarming number! I can't understand how people who fancy themselves as a "pro" still don't know how to assemble a press kit and make a professional presentation. I applaud YOU for taking the time to read this book, so you don't make those mistakes with your career.

The materials in the press kit should be as follows:

- Cover Letter

- CD

- Biography

- Fact Sheet

- 8x10 B&W photo

- Press Clippings

- Tour Itinerary

All of those items must be housed in a two-pocket folder. Do not send all of these materials floating around loose in an envelope. Be sure and order professional B&W photos. I've seen enough pictures copied on a crappy home printer to last a lifetime. Visit www.abcpictures.com and check out what they have to offer. I've hired them for many years and they have always done a great job for my projects.

Preparing your CD and press kit correctly is money well spent. An unprofessional product tells the recipient that you are not serious about your career. If you are not willing to take the time and effort to polish up your presentation, why should they feel confident investing their time and money into you? Your project's success will largely be determined by how much effort you, as the artist, are putting into it.

COVER LETTER

Begin by drafting a cover letter. Explain to the recipient why you are contacting them, who you are and what you are looking for. For example, if you are asking them for a recording contract, a gig or radio airplay, make that clear in your letter.

Make sure your contact information is on the cover letter. I receive packages each week that have no mention of the sender's phone number, mailing address or e-mail address. As I mentioned earlier, don't make that same mistake! If the recipient loves your music, they may not be able to track you down easily. Busy executives won't even bother searching for your contact information on the Internet. You'll have sealed their impression of you by failing to include your contact information.

Don't be overly boastful or cocky in the letter. Keep it short, professional and to the point. Try not to use strong adjectives such as "brilliant," "genius," "amazing" and so on in the cover letter and biography. Sometimes letters too hyped up make industry people cringe. Your credibility may be harmed if the music doesn't live up to your big words. You have every right to speak highly of yourself, but try to do it in a professional and humble manner.

At the end of the letter, make sure you let the recipient know that you will be following up on the package in a week or so and that you are looking forward to hearing their thoughts about the music. If you are not the best letter writer, don't hesitate to seek help from a friend who is good in the department. Clear wording, accurate spelling and good grammar all paint a picture of your project. Make it a favorable picture.

The CD

If your goal is to sell CDs at shows and use another portion of your order to approach music industry executives, please do yourself a favor and order professionally manufactured compact discs. Don't burn a stack of CDs in your basement, slap a sticker on it and call it your demo. I suggest a 4 song CD, with professional photography and graphic design. That way as you approach various industry pros, you'll have a product that looks like you mean business.

The only time I advocate "homemade" CDs is for songwriters who are simply looking to place songs with established artists or with TV/Film executives. Then it's acceptable to burn a two or three song CD while preparing a neat and professional label on your computer. Don't forget to include lyrics sheets when shopping individual songs.

A busy industry executive will not have the time to hunt around your entire CD to find out which songs are the most radio friendly and commercial. You may even consider placing a small sticker on every CD that is sent to industry pros, pointing out the three strongest songs on the disc.

Biography

The Biography is a very important tool in the press kit. It should center on the artist's hometown, musical background and training, the project's history and formation details, musical genre, accomplishments, early influences, touring experience, current activities and goals. It could also include some interesting or fun facts about the group or its members. Make sure the content is informative and interesting to the reader. It should also contain contact and Web site information. Make sure your double check the spelling before printing out the final product.

People who eventually read your bio may include record

company and radio station executives, managers, publishers, booking agents and people in the print media. This one page document should quickly inform the recipient about the artist, and do it in a clear, factual, efficient and entertaining way. Have someone else read it too, so you can get a second opinion before printing out a stack of copies.

As I mentioned, bios should be kept to one page and printed on high quality paper. Type it up on a home computer and print on a really good printer. Choose a font that is easy to read. Never release a handwritten biography or type it on an old-fashioned typewriter. Don't print bios if your printer's ink cartridge is on the way out. Fading bios look terrible.

You could also hire a company that specializes in designing biographies and press kits, if you feel that you need some professional help. Your press kit and demo are there to create excitement and interest in your act. This is not an area where you should cut corners.

FACT SHEET

A one page "Fact Sheet" (see sample on page 154) is another important document to include in your press kit, in addition to the official Biography. The bio is the more detailed of the two. The fact sheet should give the reader a decent profile about the artist in a few quick seconds. Use short sentences that are concise and easy to understand. Magazine and newspaper writers often turn to an artist's fact sheet for supplemental information before or after conducting an interview or to double check the accuracy of names, dates and other information.

I suggest that you keep it to one page and include information such as hometown, musical style, band member's names and instruments, management and record company information, a few interesting facts about the artist and complete contact information.

Some busy industry people go to the fact sheet first to learn basic information, before reading the more in-depth biography. So be sure and do a good job with this document.

Don't forget to include info such as the title of your CD, the genre of the music, upcoming tour dates and which are the "singles" on the record.

You should use bullet points to make it easier to read. List the call letters, city and state of every radio station that played your music and the names & locations of every club you performed in. Pull the best line or two from several of your reviews and add those to the Fact Sheet as well. This is an opportunity to toot your own horn. Don't be shy! Let people see how much you've accomplished.

PHOTOS

You cannot underestimate the importance of an outstanding picture. A great promotional photo can tell the public a great deal about your sound, image, personality and direction. Don't be afraid to get creative!

If you need a professional photographer to take your pictures, go for it. This is another area where you should not cut corners. Their experience can help you when it comes to lighting, positioning, and backgrounds for your photo shoot. These pictures are going to be used on your CD, fliers, Web site and posters. They must be great!

When interviewing photographers, try to hire someone with experience in working with musicians and music groups. You should also request to look at their portfolio to see what they've done with other artists. If someone's total focus is on weddings or corporate shoots, they may not be the best choice for you. Take your time and chose the right person for your project.

A black and white, 8x10 photo is a must for your press kit. The artist's name and contact information should be typeset on each picture. Photos are a way for artists to demonstrate the marketability of their image. Musicians must be able to sell themselves through the images created by their look. It's important to choose pictures from the shoot that make the artist look their best, while conveying a strong message about their style and personality.

Contact www.abcpictures.com for information on their

services. They do a great job with 8x10 photo reproduction and offer many other really nice promotional materials. You should also ask your photographer if he or she wants their name listed on the side of the 8x10, in the border, in a small font.

If someone not affiliated with the artist is in any of the photos, be sure to have them sign a model release form. Your photographer should be able to supply you with that document. If someone in the background will not sign the model release, then do not use that picture. Wait until they move out of the way before taking the photo. The photo must only feature the artist, not strangers who happen to be walking by. If you have questions about people's right to privacy, please consult your attorney.

Long before the photo shoot begins, you should put everything in writing, including the fee, the shoot's time, day and location and who owns the photographs at the conclusion of the photo shoot. The photographer may also add in clauses regarding travel and film processing fees.

In most cases, the photographer will want to remain as owner of the pictures. For a specified fee and for specified uses, you will be able to use the photos. For example, your deal may allow you the rights to use the pictures on your CDs, promo photos, Web site and posters. If down the road, you decide to use a picture from that shoot on a T-shirt, you will have to contact the photographer and work out a deal for those specific rights. In other words, when a recording artist hires a photographer, the artist is allowed to "lease" the various photos for certain agreed upon uses. The artist cannot use the pictures from the shoot any way that they want, without working out the terms and the fee with the photographer in advance.

Some photographers will allow the artist to purchase all of the rights to the photos taken at a photo shoot, but this could be costly upfront. If the asking price is fair and you, as the artist, would like total control and ownership of the photos, then you may want to explore this possibility, if the photographer is even open to that sort of arrangement.

PRESS CLIPPINGS

If a newspaper or music publication has printed favorable reviews or articles about your act, you should also include a copy of that in your press kit. A positive write-up will show that the print media is interested and impressed by your act. This will also show record companies that you are making a name for yourself with the press. These are called clips, reprints, or sometimes tearsheets.

I suggest that you include two to four of these clips in each press kit, if available. They may be a combination of interviews, articles, CD reviews or even reviews of your live show. They should each be photocopied on a clean sheet of quality paper and include the publication's masthead at the top/center of the page, along with the date it appeared in the publication.

If you are fortunate enough to have five or more pieces to choose from, I suggest you narrow it down to the four most favorable ones that came from the biggest, most well known publications. If you ever receive a really negative CD review, with not one positive comment in the entire piece, I suggest that you don't include that one. It may sound obvious, but I have received many press kits that featured one or two really bad CD reviews – and for some reason, the artist put those in the press kit too. Don't do that.

OTHER MATERIALS

Another valuable item to have in your press kit is a list of your performances, both recent and upcoming. Bookings are evidence that you are gaining stage experience, building a fan base, and generating income. It is also important to note if you have ever performed on the same bill with a nationally recognized act. The Fact Sheet is the correct place to display this information.

When unsigned acts are hired to open up for a national, signed act, usually the most well known up and coming act in a given market will get that coveted slot. So it tells industry people that your music is good and that you have a solid following in that area.

Often, I get asked if lyric sheets are important to include in a press kit, if the lyrics are not listed in the inner sleeve of the CD. I feel that if the words are hard to understand because of the vocalist's singing style, then it would be a good idea to include lyric sheets in the press kit. I'm not sure how many industry pros will be reading through the lyrics anyway. It seems that most people pop in the CD, check out a few songs while reading the Bio and some of the press, then move on to the next package. If you really feel that you want the lyrics to be part of the presentation, add the lyric sheets. In you are a songwriter shopping songs to established artists, with the intention of placing material with someone else, always enclose lyrics.

Many artists ask me if a visual presentation is an important item to have in their press kit. Quite often, the decision comes down to finances. A video replicated onto a DVD is an effective promotional tool. I'm not talking about a standard MTV-style music video here. I will cover those later in this book. I'm referring to a 4 to 8 minute demonstration video that includes live footage, candid footage of the artist in the studio and interviews with the artist. I'm sure you get the idea...

With the increasing importance of an artist's visual appeal, a professional video is not a bad thing to have. The footage can be used on the artist's Web site and a DVD can be included in each press kit sent out to key industry executives.

You may even choose to put the edited video footage directly on your CD with the music. I've seen more and more artists doing that lately. It allows industry executives the opportunity to not only hear their music, but to watch a video of the artist in action. If someone likes your music but does not have the opportunity to see you perform live, an enhanced CD or DVD can be quite helpful. If you have a professional MTV-style video in your arsenal, that's even better!

Should you decide to have a visual presentation in your press kit, it should be between four and eight minutes in length. It may show the artist performing live, depict a story line, or be a combination of the two. Some interview footage would also be a nice plus if possible. This is definitely an area where a little creativity and vision can go a long way. And with the cost of cameras and editing software being quite reasonable, many artists are making and editing their own low budget videos.

Another great item to have in your arsenal would be color posters. Posters can be used to promote upcoming gigs. Make sure a white box, around 3 to 4 inches, is at the bottom of it, so you can take a marker and neatly write in information such as a performance's date and time. Mail those posters, with the info written in already, to all of the venues you will be playing, four to five weeks in advance if possible. Send two to each venue. More if it's a really big place. Ask the person who booked you there to please hang up the poster(s) up as soon as possible after they receive the package.

Don't fold the posters and mail those in that manner. When they are unpacked, the posters will have an unsightly seam where they were folded. Go to an office supply story and purchase some mailing tubes.

You can also sell autographed posters to fans on your Web site. And make sure that every store carrying your CD has a poster, especially if you have a gig coming up in that market.

ADDITIONAL ADVICE

Never "shotgun" a press kit to a music industry professional. To shotgun a package means you found an industry executive's address somewhere and mailed them a package without first contacting them for permission. You should always call or e-mail first and ask if you could submit a package.

After introducing yourself, briefly explain what you do, and what you are looking for from this particular person. Your call may be as simple as, "Hello Mr. Smith, my name is John/Jane Musician, and I'm in a rock band based in Boston. We have a demo and are interested in sending you a package. What is your submission policy?"

You may only be able to get through to a receptionist, but be polite to everyone you speak with. This may sound extremely basic, but you wouldn't believe the number of people who are rude on the phone or fail to find out someone's submission policy before mailing a package.

As you or your team members begin to send your CD around to record companies, music publishers, radio stations magazines and other music industry professionals, the key word is patience. You'll be submitting to extremely busy people, so don't be offended if it takes them a month or longer to respond after you sent the package. If you are patient and polite, the listener may be more likely to accept another demo from you in the future. Don't let your disappointment show and keep you from securing a continuing business relationship.

Listen to their constructive criticism objectively and try to learn from it. Songwriting is a craft that you should always be trying to improve. Music is very much a "people" business. If you are difficult to deal with, industry professionals will not be willing to help you. You do not want to get a reputation as rude or unprofessional. Being considerate and gracious will pay off in the long run. Be sure to act polite to everyone, not just to the executives. Today's assistants are tomorrow's big shots in many cases. Always remember that.

You also have to keep in mind that demos sent in by big name lawyers, agents, managers and music publishers are going to get listened to ahead of your unsolicited tape. These days, most record companies will not even accept unsolicited demos. So you may need a reputable and connected manager, agent or lawyer on your team when you are ready to begin the process of shopping to labels and publishers.

Without the right knowledge and contacts, it is not easy getting a demo into the right hands. In many cases, a demo probably won't get beyond their mail room if it's not sent in by someone who already has a professional relationship with that label or publisher.

Unfortunately a large part of the music business involves rejection. Songwriters and artists have to learn how to deal with it quite often. There are no ways of getting around this concept. Even if you are fortunate enough to get your demo onto the right desk, they will often only listen to it for a minute or two before making a decision. If the first song impresses them, they may listen to a portion of another song. The point is you don't get much time, so you better capture their interest fast.

You put your heart, soul and money into that recording. Your calls are being ignored, or you're receiving cold, generic rejection letters. You have to remember that A&R representatives have to tell people "no" all day long. It's not fun turning people down. But their livelihood depends on picking the right songs and the right artists. They do not have an easy job, believe me.

One of the most difficult things I have to do each week is passing on projects when someone wants to hire me for a campaign, but I'm not confident in their music. It's my pleasure to review every CD that comes into my office. I really do listen to each and every submission. I take notes and then pass my thoughts along to the artist. I can only represent a small number of people who send in a package, but I enjoy giving everyone feedback and direction.

I would say that about 98% of the artists that I pass on welcome my honest assessment and seem to appreciate my advice and guidance. Many use those comments to improve and wind up approaching me months later with new and improved material. It's great to see their growth and development. Some have actually improved to the point that they literally became a client.

But now and then someone gets a bit angry if I pass on them and feel the need to tell me that "I'm making a mistake" and "how can I not hear hits on their CD" and that "they'll be as big as The Beatles in a few years." Blah, blah, blah! I had a caller tell me one time that their mother said they were a musical genius. After hearing the demo, I did not agree with her. Not even a little bit. Perhaps "junior's" Mom should start a label for his group.

I'm sorry some people are disappointed if I don't recognize their "genius." But I'm pretty confident that if the next McCartney or Bono came across my desk, I'd recognize it all by myself.

People have to understand, once you're truly on the inside of the music business, it's a small world. The big players know the other big players and if you don't keep up the quality, you'll be sent packing fast. You can go from the major leagues down to the minors really quick.

For me to call my contacts at a radio station, or a label or a magazine to aggressively pitch a new client, I have to have complete confidence in the music and in the artist behind it. Because when that CD arrives a few days later, the executive better love it, or the next time, he or she may not accept a package from me. If it appears that I'm peddling average music – not great music – the open doors will start closing in a hurry.

So even if an A&R executive or a program director is not ready to jump up and down in ecstasy every single time I send over a package, to keep those contacts alive and well, I had better be putting something amazing in that envelope or I won't even bother. As long as the quality is there, their doors will remain open to me and thus to my clients through their alliance with me.

Before a record company is going to invest time and money in a song or project, they have to be sure that it's the right one for them. A person's job can be on the line if they make a poor business decision. Try to learn from their constructive criticism, and keep working on your songs. Give them a reason to say yes.

THE ADVISORS

Personal managers, lawyers, and booking agents can be very instrumental in advancing your career. Assembling the right advisors can often be the difference between success and failure for an artist. Qualities to consider include: experience, contacts, knowledge, enthusiasm, competence, personality, fees and commissions.

Years ago, talented acts would often be discovered by a record company executive or a producer with strong A&R contacts. The artist would be developed, recorded and then eventually marketed to consumers.

These days, most artists are presented to record company executives through a manager, lawyer, agent, producer, or publisher. By the time that they are even heard by an A&R rep, the artist should have already been developed, recorded a demo and created a significant buzz.

If a label hears about your act from a few different sources, that may really peak their interest. Most record companies are now counting on the artist's advisors to groom and develop them long before they offer a deal. This has made the importance of personal managers, lawyers, agents and booking agents greatly increase over the years.

THE MANAGER

A skilled personal manager can be a tremendous asset to the artist's career. On the other hand, an incompetent manager can actually harm the artist. A manager will often make a great deal of decisions with, or on the artist's behalf. You need someone who knows the music business inside and out. One must be very selective in choosing their personal manager.

The majority of personal managers receive a 15% to 20% percent commission, and their contracts usually last between one to five years. Before signing any contract, make sure that you have an entertainment lawyer review it on your behalf.

Most personal managers help their artists choose which songs to include on the demo. As you know, songs are the most important component of the entire package. Hopefully, you will have a manager who has a good ear for hit material. If outside songwriters are needed, your manager can contact music publishers and song writers for tunes that would be suitable for your project.

When you're ready for a producer and a recording studio, your manager should help you find the right people and setting. An artist and his manager must be able to successfully communicate with each other. It is vital that your manager understands your vision, so he or she can find the right producer for the project.

If you eventually sign with a record company, your manager should be in regular contact with them on your behalf. Your manager must make sure that the promotional and marketing people are properly handling their respective responsibilities regarding your project. Your manager should also be in touch with the label regarding various business and creative decisions that come up.

Managers also interview and hire photographers, publicists, and other music industry professionals for or with you. This allows the artist to concentrate more intently on the music. A manager should also assist with polishing up your entire act, including your image and your live show.

You should look for a manager who has genuine enthusiasm

for your career. You also want someone who truly believes in you and understands your goals, artistic vision and direction. They are going to be your number one cheerleader, so you will want someone who is really excited about your project. Your career is going to be in their hands in many ways. Make sure that you believe in their abilities as much as they believe in yours.

Some up-and-coming artists are managed by sharp, young people who make up for their inexperience through hard work and business savvy. If this is the only person you can find, then the decision is up to you. However, my recommendation is to look for someone who has management experience and solid industry contacts.

Many experienced personal managers are talented negotiators with excellent business skills. They often have a wide range of contacts throughout the music industry. Our industry is propelled by networking, and the concept of "it's who you know, not what you know" rings true on a daily basis. Record companies are also more at ease when they see that an artist's career is being guided by a professional whom they know and respect.

When the situation is right, a personal manager can be a wonderful asset to a recording artist. The manager becomes an advisor, an ally, a negotiator, a promoter and most importantly, a confidant. Your manager should do everything in his or her power to advance your career, while allowing you the luxury of concentrating on writing, recording, rehearsing and performing.

One of the key elements in a successful artist/manager relationship revolves around trust. If trust is not there, people begin to look elsewhere and things begin to crumble from the inside. The parties must also share the same vision. Everyone has to agree and want the same thing for the artist's career. Open lines of communication are crucial in this area. Unrealistic expectations will do no one any good.

Make sure that you enjoy and celebrate any positive goals that have been reached. An impromptu party to celebrate a big achievement is a nice reward for everyone on the team and encourages future success. A good manager will embrace your positive contributions to the project. Sometimes people are so focused on the future, they forget to enjoy the present moment a little bit.

THE ATTORNEY

Another important advisor is your entertainment attorney. It's very important to have an entertainment lawyer when you need legal or career advice relating to the music industry. They can help you with general legal issues and handle all of your contract related needs.

If you are given a recording contract, a personal management agreement, or anything else related to the entertainment industry, hire someone to review your paperwork who deals with those issues every day. I feel that the lawyer should be the first person that you bring on board as your "team" is created.

Try to hire someone who really knows the music business. Entertainment lawyers know what the industry standards are when they review or negotiate a contract for you. They know what deal points and percentages are fair for their clients. If someone has no music industry related experience because they concentrate on another area of law, they may not know all of the nuances that are found in music-related contracts.

You should never sign a contract without having a lawyer advise you. The music industry is filled with horror stories about people who signed things without legal assistance and ended up paying for that mistake many times over.

I know it may sound like simple advice, but I always here stories of people who signed a contract without the guidance of an attorney, "to save a few bucks" and wound up very sorry they made that move. Don't ever tell me that you have no money for a lawyer. If you need to come up with a few hundred dollars to potentially prevent yourself from years of problems, then find a way to get the cash together. If you sign the wrong document, or make a bad business decision, it will cost you far more in the long run.

Many entertainment lawyers have strong contacts with record company A&R executives, music publishers and record producers. Artist shopping is a service that many can offer to highly qualified candidates. This means that for a fee generally ranging from $1,500 to upwards of $5,000, the lawyer will send your demo and press kit to his or her A&R contacts in an effort to get you a recording contract. The lawyer will conduct all initial correspondence, then follow up on the packages and update you according to the terms of your attorney-client agreement.

If the lawyer is successful in securing a deal, he or she usually receives a commission based upon the initial advance and/or the signing bonus. Some even ask for a percentage of future royalties. There are many variations on fees, commissions and bonuses, so I suggest that you check around.

Some lawyers concentrate on contracts, career guidance and other transactional services and do not shop artists. Speak to several people and decide which fee structure and person is best for your needs. Don't be afraid to call around and ask some questions. Be sure that your call is brief, polite and to the point. You will be calling people who are extremely busy.

When it comes to other services, such as contract drafting, document reviewing, deal negotiating or career guidance most lawyers charge an hourly fee ranging from $200 to $500. Some will charge a flat rate for a specific task, such as preparing a contract or letter for you.

You may also choose to discuss a retainer with the attorney. Generally, a retainer is when the client pays a law firm a monthly, quarterly or annual fee upfront and then hourly expenses for services rendered are deducted from the money you paid in advance. The lawyer is then available to give the client legal advice and professional services throughout the agreed upon time period as long as money still remains in reserve.

For example, if you have a $1,500 dollar retainer with your attorney and their hourly rate is $200 and services that you requested took three hours, then $200 x 3 = $600. Therefore you would have used up $600 of your retainer and would still have $900 left in your "account."

Most entertainment lawyers will not work on complete spec deals. This basically means providing various legal services for free until the artist becomes a success and can then afford to pay for the accrued services. It happens occasionally I'm sure, but with so few artists who actually make it big, if professionals did everything on spec for everyone, they could not afford to remain in business. Lawyers and other professionals have large overhead costs, such as employee salaries, rent, health insurance, advertising, office equipment and other general business expenses. Take that into consideration the next time you are thinking about hiring any highly trained professional.

You'll be working closely with your lawyer, so try to find someone that has a personality you like, in addition to experience and contacts. It also helps to find someone who is enthusiastic about your music. If they are going to shop your CD around, they should sincerely believe in the music.

Most record companies refuse unsolicited packages and only accept demos from lawyers, agents, managers, publishers and record producers that they have a professional relationship with. Once again, contacts play a tremendous role. How can you expect to get a deal if nobody ever hears your demo?

The chances that an A&R rep will walk into your neighborhood bar on a Tuesday night and see you performing live is not very likely. This is especially true if you don't live in a major music city such as New York, Los Angeles or Nashville.

Many up-and-coming acts cannot find an experienced and competent manager who is willing to work with them. Therefore, the artist has nobody knowledgeable to direct their career. In situations like this, an entertainment lawyer can fill this void and guide the artist through the often confusing music business.

The Booking Agent

The "booking agent" is another important advisor on your team. Their primary duty is to secure well paying gigs for you. Some booking agents will also help promote and advertise concerts and personal appearances.

You already know the importance of playing live and how it relates to increasing your buzz and income. It's very important to secure a booking agent who has contacts at the venues in your region so they can get you steady, paying work.

Unsigned acts can perform at a variety of venues including clubs, colleges, festivals, hotels, casinos, restaurants, record stores, book stores and so on. Most booking agents receive a 5% to 10% percent commission for the concerts that they secure for you.

Record companies are impressed when an act already has a booking agent. They know that acts who are out there performing regularly are probably going to sell more records and merchandise than artists who are not performing as often.

When an experienced professional is arranging your live performances, a label is confident that record sales will increase due to the higher exposure. I often suggest to artists that they should get their press kit and demo to booking agents in their region and start building relationships with those people. Even if they are not ready to sign you today, keep the right agencies up to date on your efforts. Eventually they may see enough progress to finally offer you a deal. Perhaps they would even offer you an opening spot on a tour with an artist already on their roster.

If you are planning a tour, an accomplished booking agent can also help you decide how much money you could expect and what markets would be most receptive to your music. When your booking agent gets an offer from a club or venue, they should contact your manager for approval before the gig is booked. This should prevent double booking or scheduling problems.

An "agent" is not to be confused with a "booking agent." I can best explain the role of an "agent" as a cross between a manager and a lawyer. They help the artist with a wide range of promotional, marketing, publicity and in some instances, legal tasks. The agent provides valuable direction, guidance, knowledge, experience and advice to the artist and their career on a regular basis. Some even quarterback the artist's entire promotional campaign.

Agents are usually skilled in numerous facets of the music business and are a big help in areas such as artist development, negotiation and general career guidance. Top agents have numerous contacts throughout the music industry and utilize those connections to help their clients. Many agents have a law degree and for whatever reason, do not choose to formally practice law. Some people are both an attorney and an agent. Agents are also common in the sports, television and film industries.

They help clients such as athletes, actors, songwriters, recording artists, composers, producers, session musicians and other industry participants with a variety of services. Many agents contribute to their clients by providing career and financial advice, reviewing contracts, negotiating deals, shopping material, securing endorsements, developing business opportunities and so on. Some people refer to their "booking agent" as their "agent" – simply as an abbreviated nickname. So try to be clear about which professional you are referring to, when speaking to others, if you are fortunate enough to have an agent and a booking agent.

PUBLICITY

Creating a buzz is a very important concept that many recording artists often misunderstand. This is an area that cannot be ignored or underestimated. Simply put, creating a buzz is an artist's ability to get their name and music out to the public. Let's explore some of the more common ways artists, managers and labels do this.

An important way to build a buzz is through favorable reviews and articles in various music publications. This is also known as a "publicity campaign" for anyone new to the game. Good press will help to spread the word about your act and will help you sell CDs — while getting more people out to your performances. All of these things will begin to come together as your name gets more recognizable throughout the local or regional music community.

The wonderful thing about publicity is there's not a high cost associated with this kind of exposure, if you do it yourself. If you can get your music into the rights hands at newspapers and magazines and they like what you're doing, your only cost to secure that article, interview or review is some time, the CD, a press kit and postage. Perhaps a few phone calls and shipping supplies as well. What are we talking here — eight bucks per package? Not a bad deal people!

If you hire a publicist, then you're looking at spending some cash. But if you do it yourself in the early days, and you secure a large interview or CD review, that chunk of the page is basically free. If you ever priced the cost of print ads, you know how expensive every inch of "real estate" in any publication is.

Most professional, accomplished publicists charge anywhere between $1,500 and $5,000 per month, plus expenses. And some have three-month minimums. So if you find someone willing to take on your project for a three-month campaign, at $1,500 per month plus expenses, you're looking at a financial commitment of at least $5,000.

Some publicists send out 100 to 200 packages during a national campaign. A number of those people use overnight shipping services. So if each package is approximately $15 and 200 CDs are sent out, you're looking at a $3,000 bill, just for shipping!

Speak with any publicist that you are considering and let them know if you have financial limitations, as a new artist. Suggest they use first class mail or two-day mail, to cut down on the expenses associated with the campaign. That alone can save you thousands of dollars during a lengthy project. There will be times when in the interest of time and to capitalize on a last minute opportunity, your PR guru may need to overnight a package. That's fine, as long as it's not done for every package. If you have the money to spend thousands on shipping fees alone, then it's up to you.

But remember that your packages will be going to people that receive dozens and dozens of packages each week. So even if your CD arrives early on a Tuesday morning, it might not be actually opened until Friday anyway. Perhaps. even the following Friday!

If you or your publicist can land a favorable article, interview, CD review or live concert review, it clearly increases your chance that consumers will purchase your record and/or attend a live show in that market. At the very minimum, you're beginning to get your name around and you've added another impressive item to your press kit.

Keep in mind that both parties to this "transaction" are benefiting. The artist benefits because they are getting coverage in the media and exposing their music to thousands of potential fans, without paying the high cost of print advertising. The writer or editor at the publication also benefits from covering the music scene. Their readers are craving information about hot new artists. Consumers love learning all they can about the people behind popular music. If newspapers and magazines do not consistently release appealing content, the public would simply not purchase that publication. Big time advertisers would obviously not spend their advertising dollars in a publication with little to no readers.

Always be polite and professional when dealing with any print media executive. If you have a good idea or angle for an article, let them know. But remember, you should not have to beg for coverage. If you have a great product and pitch it properly, that should be enough to begin creating a mutually rewarding relationship with a writer or editor.

Music magazines, newsweeklies, lifestyle magazines, industry trade magazines, daily newspapers and fanzines are all great publications to contact. Many of the top, national magazines also have great Web sites that provide coverage to recording artists, in the form of CD reviews and interviews.

Online Webzines are also becoming more popular and influential. The coverage you receive from the print media will help you strengthen your press kit. College newspapers are another outlet for you to contact. Quite often, those campus publications will take the time to review a local or touring artist's demo. Local newspapers usually have a music or entertainment section that can be useful for your publicity needs as well.

Underground music fanzines are a great way to get coverage for your act. They are always eager to cover up-and-coming artists and are read by a large number of music fans. Many of these music publications circulate around the world, while others concentrate on certain regions. Be sure to find out about a fanzine's distribution so you'll know what areas will be exposed to your music.

Fanzines will often print your contact information or Web site so people can join your mailing list or order a CD. Try to contact every publication that you think would be able to give you coverage. If anyone favorably reviews your CD or writes an article about your project, make sure to send a thank you card or e-mail. If you ever seek additional coverage in the future, you will be remembered as polite and professional. Print Ads

Print ads can often be expensive in daily newspapers, but many of the local and regional music publications have reasonable rates on third and quarter of the pages ads and some even offer smaller ads, about the size of a business card. I always felt that Friday was the best day for musicians to run ads to promote their shows. Friday is the day when many people grab the local music paper to see who's performing in the area that night and on Saturday evening too. So you'll get more music fans seeing your ad on a Friday, because many people will be actively looking for weekend gig information.

As you price your ads, try to avoid paying the full price on the rate card. If you're polite and professional, you should be able to negotiate a 10% to 15% discount off of the quoted price. (Especially if you are booking several ads at one time.) Some publications charge extra to design the ad for you, if you don't already have that task completed. Let the salesperson know that you are an independent artist on a tight budget and again, attempt to haggle the price down a bit.

You should also make sure the sales executive at the publication knows where you want the ad placed. If you're promoting your gigs for next weekend, placing your ad in the sports or business section is probably not a great idea. Make it clear to the salesperson that you want your ad in the music or entertainment section. (If it's more of a daily newspaper or general interest magazine.) If they entire publication is about music, then request that your ad be placed in the section that focuses on upcoming concerts and venues that offer live entertainment.

If you know someone who's talented in graphic art and design, get the specs and have your friend design the ad. I remember booking a series of $75 ads for a client once and the publication wanted an additional $100 just to design it! Fortunately, the artist had a friend who was skilled in that area and did it as a favor.

Don't forget that you're in the 'exciting and dynamic music business. Make sure your ads reflect that. If your ad looks like the local burger joint, you will not catch as many eyes as you are hoping to. Make sure that all of your print ads include your Web site address. People can and will go there to learn more about you and to hear some music samples.

Don't make the mistake of cutting corners with your ad's design. Consumers will judge your project by what they read and see. If your copy and design are poorly done, it will be a reflection on you and ultimately your music. Try to have a catchy headline and if possible, a nice bold border all the way around the ad. Those are simple techniques that will make the ad stand out more.

If the publication offers to word the ad (the copy) on your behalf, you should politely decline. If they do it, you run the risk of your ad sounding too much like the others in that issue. Most writers have a certain style and you want to be original. If grammar and spelling isn't your bag, find a friend who's willing to help you.

Studies show that the frequency of ads is important in getting consumers to respond. So try to budget your money accordingly. For example, instead of buying two consecutive issue full page ads in a monthly publication, I suggest that you book eight consecutive quarter page ads. Now you'll be seen for eight months in a row, rather than only two. You're ultimately spending the same amount of money, but having a much longer impact on consumers.

LIVE PERFORMANCES

I've always felt that live performances are a great way to promote an artist and to sell CDs and merchandise. A solid live show gets people excited about an artist. They will tell their friends, and over time, you should be drawing a larger crowd with each passing show.

It's also an opportunity for people to join your mailing list.
The more names and e-mail addresses that you can collect the
better. These days, A&R reps often ask how many people are
on an artist's list, in an effort to gauge the size of their fan base.
Radio promotion is another great way to promote and market
your group. I will cover touring and radio promotion in much
more detail, later in this book.

Considering the onslaught of product released to the
music/video market each month worldwide, it is crucial to
ensure the visibility of each project. The prospects for the
financial success of an album can be increased through the
establishment of proper promotion, publicity and marketing
budgets. However, without the dollars necessary to execute
lofty campaigns, success is not easy to achieve.

RADIO PROMOTION

Despite the fact that radio is no longer the sole influence on record sales, (sharing the honor now with music videos), it is still extremely crucial in the promotion of music. The ultimate importance of radio airplay is quite clear. Consumers hear music on the radio and if they like it enough, many will eventually purchase the CD.

When discussing radio promotion, the most common words you will hear are format and demographic. The "format" simply means the genre of music a given station is playing. It may be rock, jazz, rap, country and so on. A demographic is a list of characteristics that define a portion of the general public. It may include a person's age, income, interests, career and location.

Corporations of all sizes spend large amounts of money each year advertising on the radio. They rely on detailed statistics and market information about their customers and about those they want to become their customers. They use radio ads as a vehicle to promote their product or service directly to the audience they are trying to reach.

For example, a high end golf resort may run ads on a jazz or classical station, while a sneaker company would most likely target rock, pop and urban stations.

With so many changes occurring in the radio industry, such as the sale of radio stations, along with the fragmentation of formats and the increasing value of video, radio promoters have been forced to realize that they must approach their projects in a far more business-like manner than they did in the past. Their focus must be very business oriented, rather than simply trying to impress music or program directors with the cool new song they are sending around the country. A record is more likely to be picked up in the bigger markets if it is already having some positive results on other stations. It's also a plus if your radio promoter can let program directors see your position on the key charts, thus showing that the record is doing well elsewhere and is worthy of airtime and attention.

Having an impressive track record of sales at the retail level is another key point that may sway a radio station to give your record a few test spins. If they grant you a few of those spins and the listeners respond with favorable calls and e-mails, it may lead to even more airplay for your record on that station.

To go from a few "test spins" to actually getting on a station's formal playlist, is not easy. A playlist is a given station's own chart, featuring the 25 to 40 records that are receiving the most airplay that week. Since most stations receive hundreds of CDs each month, it's not easy to crack the top twenty. The competition is fierce. Securing airplay at college radio is far more difficult than in the past, with the major labels and top indie labels all servicing the college stations with their product on a regular basis these days. If you are a rock group, for example, you may be competing with the biggest names in your genre for one of those coveted slots. You better bring a great record to the table if you expect to be successful.

I find myself being an optimist and if your record really is great and you have a top radio promoter on your team, I feel that you will get meaningful spins and the attention that you are seeking from the radio community. College radio may be your only radio outlet in the early, unsigned days. But don't underestimate the power of that medium. College students are often very big music fans and if they embrace your record in large numbers, the sky is the limit.

But even at college radio, "who you know" is very, very important. Personal relationships with radio station program and music directors are the main reason unsigned, independent and major label artists hire radio promoters. Overwhelmed by new songs and new records each week, program directors are inclined to assist those with whom they are already familiar and friendly. The value of those professional relationships cannot be underestimated. Most indie promoters position themselves and focus within a specific music genre. So they have strong ties in the genre that they specialize in.

College students, who have always been a large portion of the target market for music products, are leading the way in the acceptance of Internet download technology. Clearly, college students are knowledgeable about digital music and are active multi-taskers. They are increasingly turning to the Internet for instant gratification in fueling their passion for music.

Two of the best known publications that track the radio charts include College Music Journal (C.M.J.) and Friday Morning Quarterback. Taking out a print ad in CMJ's weekly trade publication is a good way to get your name out there just before you launch a radio campaign. Radio personnel read that magazine cover to cover each and every week. If your CD winds up on their desk a few days after they saw your ad, chances are the name will ring a bell. They may open it up right then and there, rather than toss it into a pile with dozens of others new arrivals. Yet again, another example of the importance of building your brand name!

Servicing "reporting stations" is very important. A reporting station is one that trade papers, magazines and tip sheet publishers correspond with each week to learn which recordings were given airplay. Information is collected and tabulated from stations around the country. It is presented to the public in the form of a chart which shows things such as the current chart position, prior chart position, the name of the artist, song, album, record label, and so on.

Commercial radio often prefers to play songs by established, popular artists. They want listeners to tune in and stay tuned in, so they can charge more for advertising. Many consumers are not interested in hearing new artists and rather hear familiar songs and well known artists. Since the radio stations want to keep their listeners happy, they gravitate to playing what people want to hear. Sadly, this attitude keeps new and emerging artists off of commercial radio more often than not.

College stations are one of the few outlets that will still play music from unsigned acts. Approaching college radio program directors either on your own or through a professional radio promoter is vital. It can be a big boost to your buzz if a large number of stations like your music and start playing it regularly. Radio promoters usually try to arrange on-air interviews and performances for the artist, when warranted. Large amounts of airplay on a given station can at times be capitalized on further, by securing a gig on or near campus.

College and public radio stations are generally not dependent on advertising revenue, so things like ratings and listener marketing statistics are not as important. They program what they like and what they feel their audience will like.

Whenever financially possible, I recommend that people hire a professional and reputable radio promotion company. If you must handle radio promotion on your own in the early days, I will offer you some insight and tips right now. Please make sure you target the correct stations before you start mailing out CDs and press kits. Sending your rock or rap album to a jazz station is a waste. And as obvious as that seems, people do it every day. Do your homework before heading to the Post Office.

Most college stations play a variety of music genres, so make it clear in your cover letter to the Music Director what your style is. You may even consider placing a small sticker on the outside of the envelope listing your genre.

Perhaps something as simple as "Enclosed – Rock Music" or "Enclosed – Jazz Music" – can point your package in the right direction upon arrival at the station.

Another good tip would be for you to remove the cellophane from the CD, so a busy radio station executive or assistant can open it and review the music quickly. While on I'm that subject, I suggest that you remove the cellophane from every CD that you sent to music industry professionals. Removing the wrapping is annoying and time consuming, especially for someone who's trying to get through dozens and dozens of packages in an afternoon.

Also, when drafting your cover letter, mention which song is the first single. Radio and record company executives don't have the time to search through your entire CD to find the most commercial and radio-friendly song.

A&R reps usually keep track of who is making progress on the college radio charts through their research departments. If they keep seeing your name in music trade magazines and on various college radio station playlists, they may start to take notice. Many college radio stations will allow acts to perform live, acoustic sets on the air. Sometimes they will even conduct in-studio interviews with unsigned acts.

If you are on a tight budget and cannot afford to hire a professional radio promoter, there are a few steps that you should take to at least have a chance for success. Initially, you should reach out to college radio stations in your region. Do your homework buy visiting their Web sites to find out if they program your genre of music. You can also find their music director's name, phone number, E-mail and mailing address.

Call the MD and introduce yourself. Make it polite and get right to the point. Practice what you want to say a few times in advance with a friend, so you have your pitch tight and ready to go. Let them know you are an independent artist, let them know where you've been performing and how many CDs you've sold to date. If you have had success with the local newspaper or any print media for that matter, mention that too.

Ask if you could submit a CD/press kit for review and how long you should wait before following up. You must also ask for their office hours or call times. In the radio world, call times are the days and times that a music director accepts follow up calls from promoters, artists, managers and labels. For example, the MD at a station in your town may only accept follow up calls on Tuesdays and Fridays between 2:00 PM and 5:00 PM. If you call at any other time, you are just wasting your time!

When you get the MD on the phone that first time, you'll have about 60 seconds to make a great impression. Know what you want to say, while being polite and professional. When you begin the follow up calls, keep that professional and thankful attitude. Find out if they received the package, did they review it yet, what are their thoughts about the music and will it be receiving airplay. You should also ask if it will be receiving an add.

Keep a list of every station that has granted your CD airplay. You can turn that information into a Radio Fact Sheet and include it in all future press kits. Use bullet points and simply list the call letters, city and state.

I prefer to launch college radio campaigns in September and January. These are the two times of year when the new semester begins on campuses across the country. During the summer, most stations have a smaller staff, some have reduced hours of operation and others even shut their doors for a few months! Not to mention that a large majority of the students are not on campus during the summer, thus decreasing the number of people that will hear your songs if you do succeed in securing airplay. I've also heard of people working college radio hard in the summer, because there is usually less competition from more established artists during those months.

For unsigned or indie label artists, I feel that college radio promotion campaigns and touring are the most important ways to promote a project. If you are successful in getting it on the air and then securing a gig in that market, you are headed in the right direction. The students who listen to college radio are usually the same people that support original music and come out to concerts at the local clubs. They also buy CDs and merchandise at these shows and happily spread the word about great new music they have discovered. If you live near a big college or major university, you better make it a high priority to get their radio station into your music and behind your project. If you can pull that alliance off, you'll be in good shape, my friend.

Another thing that I want to mention regarding college radio is respect. I have spoken to many artists who are in their late 20's and older, who for some reason resent having to be polite to the college students they speak with at the radio stations. Especially the ones who "pass" on their record! I guess it bothers their ego to suck up to someone younger in their pursuit of radio airplay.

Be nice to people. It's just the right thing to do. Be respectful, polite and professional, especially when you are calling a complete stranger and asking them for a favor! I'm sure you're the picture of polite behavior at all times – but I wanted to make it clear anyway.

And for those of you out there that need even more convincing on why they should be nice to college radio personnel – remember this – many of the people you are now dealing with will go on to full time jobs in the music business. Some will wind up at commercial radio, some at record companies and others at music publications. People remember jerks, as much as they remember cool people. Always keep that in mind.

Since I do college radio promotion every day, I've seen dozens of examples where someone I was dealing with at a station later went on to an A&R job at a major label, an MD job at a top commercial station, or a became a writer at a well known music publication. They remembered me as being professional and courteous. It goes without saying that their door remained opened to me and ultimately to my clients.

Another important point to keep in mind... If a station passes on your CD today, don't think it's the end of the world. Many times I have had a station pass on a client's CD for whatever subjective reason – and then pick it up later, once the artist has more press or success at radio elsewhere, or had a big gig in that market added to their tour itinerary. Don't burn bridges or close doors behind yourself.

Most industry professionals have their own philosophy when it comes to radio promotion. Guess what, I do too! Of course, everyone who launches a radio campaign hopes that 100% of the stations serviced love the record and will play it over and over. But since that's a rare event, especially for unsigned or independent artists, how do you keep your sanity when not everyone loves your music?

I like to start by setting realistic goals. Most radio stations receive a ton of CDs each and every week, especially in January and September. So you're competing with literally hundreds of artists, if not thousands, including many backed by the major labels, for a small slice of that coveted, sweet airtime. Let's assume that an artist based in New Jersey mails out 100 packages all across the country on his own, without the assistance of a professional radio promoter. "Johnny Rockstar" then starts his follow up calls from Maine to California. Johnny gets the MD from a station in San Francisco on the phone and brings a healthy dose of smooth talking to the conversation.

Johnny's polite, humble and may have even washed his hair that morning for the big occasion. He clearly means business! He starts by asking if the CD was reviewed yet and if it will be, or is, receiving airplay. The MD may have even given the CD a quick review by then. But since Johnny isn't performing in San Fran anytime soon and has no press at that point in the market and doesn't have records in stores there, the MD may not be willing to squeeze Mr. Rockstar into their playlist.

So Johnny may be told it's a pass! After anyone has twenty disappointing calls in a row like that, my guess is their stomach won't be having its finest moment. But let's remain positive and forget for a moment, just how difficult securing radio really is.

However, if the MD liked the record, and Johnny came off as professional and sincere, the station may be willing to grant the CD's first single a few test spins over the course of the next two or three weeks. Johnny may even get a polite invitation to "keep the station posted" if he books a gig in town or if the local newspaper does a feature article down the road a bit.

Congrats Mr. Rockstar, you have now successfully added another radio station to your Fact Sheet! Your next move should be to send a Thank You card to the Music Director, yet another classy move that will be appreciated and remembered by the radio executives.

If the artist's eventual goal is to secure a record deal, then they really have scored a victory in this example. They secured airplay and the exposure that comes with that coupe. They have more ammo for their press kit to show labels, managers, venues, the press and other industry executives that the music is being taken seriously - and in some way, it's being embraced. It's a good start. You just have to duplicate that success in many markets across the country before you have earned the right to call your radio campaign a true winner.

In these early days, secure all of the spins you can get and keep that info handy so executives can see your track record. Add the list of radio stations playing your record to your Web site and ask people to call or e-mail requests for your song. Keep your name on the mind of the MDs across the country. Signed artists often bombard radio stations with song requests and to build and maintain a radio buzz, along with name recognition. It's often through the efforts of Street Teams. I'm sure you're familiar with that term. If you can't afford to hire a professional Street Team, then be your own and start working. But do it in a professional, intelligent manner, or radio stations will quickly realize it's the artist and not really music fans making all of the requests. Be smart and don't embarrass yourself.

As you progress up the ladder, you should then have greater expectations from a radio campaign. In each market that your team is targeting, you will aim to secure press, a gig, a presence at retail and significant, meaningful airplay, also known as heavy rotation. Make sure you continue to add any new stations to your Fact Sheet. Success at radio is not easy, so if you are fortunate enough to earn that, make sure industry people are aware of your achievement.

If you get to the point where you have 50 or more stations playing your CD, you may want to draft a "Radio Fact Sheet" - so you can fit all of the radio information on one page. The original Fact Sheet discussed earlier would remain focused strictly on the artist's general information, a list of venues where you performed, statistics, awards, press quotes/blurbs and other successful accomplishments.

"Statistics" would include CD sales, average number of monthly visitors to your Web site, number of fans on you e-mail list, number of friends on MySpace and the average attendance at gigs.

I know from first hand experience, the first time you hear a DJ announce the next song and it's your project – and the sound of that tune fills your car... WOW, it's a magical moment! I hope that you will experience it some day, if you haven't already.

RADIO ADVERTISING

Some college and non-commercial radio stations offer very affordable advertising rates. In the radio world, commercials are referred to as "spots." I've seen 60 second spots for as low as $10 each in some markets! It's a great way to get a snippet of your music on the radio and with well written copy (a/k/a "The Script") – you can plug upcoming shows, your Web site and even the name of the local store that's selling the CD.

Some stations offer 30 second spots, but I feel you need the full 60 to really get all of your information across while still leaving some time for the music to be playing without any distractions. If you have access to studio equipment, you could probably make your own radio commercial and save even more money. Especially if you or someone you know has a great speaking voice.

I suggest having the spot open up with several seconds of your music, cued to the chorus of your best song of course! Then the voice over personality kicks in with the information for the listeners. (The music is still playing while he or she speaks, but it's simply pulled back in the mix a bit.) Then after the copy is read, bring the level of the music back up front and center. Allow the last seconds of the spot be filled with your wonderful music.

Make sure you repeat your name and Web site slowly and clearly several times. Repetition is crucial in radio advertising because people are often not totally concentrating. They may be at work, or on the phone or driving. Make sure your repeat your key info often. As you put together your radio spot campaign with the salesperson at the station, try to get as many commercials as you can for your budget and spread those out. I'd rather see you run 4 spots a day for one month, then 8 spots a day for two weeks. Everyone has their own media buying philosophy, but I feel pretty strongly that repetition over time really drives a message home with consumers.

So repeat the key information often in your spot and run the spots often. Again, don't forget the importance of repetition in radio advertising. The same thing goes for radio spots as it does for print ads… negotiate a better price then the one they initially put on the table. (Especially if you have $1,000 or more to spend at a given station.)

Since you're promoting a music act, I also suggest securing time slots between 3PM and Midnight. During the day, most of the people you will be targeting are in school or work and not near a radio! If the sales rep uses the term "drive times" – they are generally referring to the morning and evening rush hours. 6:00 a.m. to 10:00 a.m. and again from 3:00 p.m. to 7:00 p.m. The drive time rates are the most expensive, since that's the time of the day when the most listeners are tuned in.

If you're really on a tight budget, but still want to run radio commercials, here's something you can try… It doesn't always work and you may not get prime slots, but keep this tactic in mind… When speaking to the sales rep, let them know you are an up-and-coming recording artist on a tight budget. Express your desire to become an advertiser with that station. Try to negotiate a discounted rate, in return you will waive your request for specific time frames.

Therefore, you would be allowing the station to run your

spot at any time they had openings to fill. It's a win-win. You get discounted commercials and they make a few bucks by filling up previously open and unsold minutes. This is especially good to try in smaller markets that are often starving for advertisers.

If you have a few bucks in your marketing and advertising budgets, you should consider experimenting with radio advertising. I've seen many clients use it to successfully promote gigs, new CDs and in-store appearances across the United States or right in their own hometown.

MUSIC VIDEOS & TELEVISION COMMERCIALS

Music Videos
Music videos became a regular part of our industry in the early 1980's with the emergence of MTV. I feel that a well done video is a wonderful way for artists to create and promote their music, their brand name and their image to music fans around the world.

Since high quality music videos are very expensive, many record companies are not so quick to pay for one for each new artist. Sometimes a label will wait to see how sales are doing at retail from other methods of promotion and marketing and then decide if a video is warranted or not.

Some record companies recoup the entire cost of a video, while many others will only recoup fifty percent, thus splitting the financial burden with the artist. Most label executives simply hope the video creates enough buzz to increase sales of the album, while promoting the artist's name and music. A video is basically an expensive promotional device.

Once a video does make it to regular rotation on MTV or VH1, they are clearly a powerful contributor in forming and projecting an artist's image and persona to the public. A few weeks of such exposure, along with the other traditional promotion and marketing methods used by major labels, can often make a new artist a household name in a few quick months. It's amazing what radio, the print media and television can do for an artist or a product. Add in a hot national tour and look out!

But since the focus of this book is on unsigned or independent label artists, not people already signed to a major label, let's examine the role and benefits of a low to medium budget video.

I feel that if an artist can afford a music video, they should do it. I think it's a very valuable tool to have at their disposal. The video can be added to your Web site, so anyone visiting can see the image and visual appeal of the artist. Even a basic, two- camera live performance video of your strongest song is a nice addition to your presentation materials. If you have the budget to add some special effects or other bells and whistles, go for it.

You should also consider pressing up a batch of the videos on DVD and including those in your press kits to select industry executives. People that receive the DVD, along with your CD and press kit could include labels, managers, booking agents, magazines, newspapers and concert venues, to name a few. This will give people the opportunity to not only hear your music, but to see you in action.

As the years go on, we are seeing audio and video being blended more and more. Any artist that can master their acting skills and look comfortable on screen, will be doing their career a big favor. And think, if you do secure a major record deal someday and you have the opportunity to film a million dollar video, you'll already have experience and confidence in your abilities.

I know companies that produce excellent music videos for the budget-conscious recording artist in the $2,500 to $5,000 range. So for less than five-thousand dollars, you could have a professional video up your sleeve. Beside the obvious promotional vehicle a video can provide for your career, getting some experience in front of a camera can also be quite beneficial. Unless you have a ton of money to spend, I really don't see the point of doing a very expensive music video if you are unsigned. Even if you spent $50,000 on a music video, where are you going to show it, aside from your Web site and in select press kits?

There are a few video channels that will play low to medium budget clips, but I don't feel that small amount of exposure warrants spending $50,000 to $100,000 of your money in the early days. I feel you are better off spending $2,000 to $5,000 on a video and using the rest of your budget on recording, pressing, radio promotion, marketing, publicity campaigns, media buying and tour support.

I spoke to a music group a few years back that had raised $50,000 from investors. They spent $40,000 of that money on a music video. I'll be the first to admit it was very well done, but it still wasn't the quality that you see on MTV. And even if it was, without a major or top indie label promoting the video, would one of the major networks even play an unsigned and completely unknown recording artist? I doubt it. So after recording this great video and then finishing up their album in the recording studio, they had no money left. The $50,000 was gone before they could even master the songs, press CDs and begin to promote and market the project. Need I mention that their investors were not very pleased with how they utilized the money? Budget wisely.

As you plan your video, some of the things you must keep in mind include:

- The budget

- The song to be featured in the video

- Director

- Producer

- Location

- Concept – Script – Story Board – Props

- Dates for shooting & editing the video

- Legal issues such as releases, permits & permission from the owner of the location

TELEVISION COMMERCIALS

Filming and airing thirty-second television commercials becomes a great way to promote a new CD or a tour, if the budget is available. Television advertising has a strong impact on consumers. How many times have you seen a fast food commercial late at night and that juicy burger looked so amazing that you were grabbing the car keys and heading out the door ten seconds later? Or you saw the iced cold beer in the hands of a supermodel sweating in the desert and you couldn't wait to guzzle down a frosty mug of lager. Hey, we've all been guilty of being swayed and influenced by commercials. They work. It's that simple, buddy. Now it's time for you to influence consumers with YOUR product!

I've seen artists and labels film and edit an impressive television commercial for under $1,500. Just make sure that it looks and sounds professional. And that includes the person's voice reading the copy and the information that is actually making up that copy. You can buy slots on local and regional cable networks for very reasonable rates. I've booked commercials for clients that were only $50 for a thirty-second slot. Sometimes the rates are far less in smaller markets and late at night. If an artist had $5,000 to spend, they could get a nice amount of commercials with that budget, if utilized properly. Prices vary by market, so do some research or hire a media buying agency to help you. Yep, I do those services as well.

Of course if costs more in major markets, and certain networks and time frames are more expensive, but with some wise decisions in choosing the markets, networks and times, you could make some serious noise and benefit from the power of television. Call around to get price quotes to run your commercial on MTV and/or VH1 in various markets. You'll be surprised how reasonable it is, especially compared to print advertising in many instances. Contact companies like Comcast & Time Warner to get information and price quotes. They offer some great deals.

Don't let a television advertising sales person try to convince you to run a portion of your commercials on networks other than the music channels without doing your homework first. If you have a large enough budget and depending on your genre, there are indeed other networks worth exploring. But make sure you are familiar with any networks the sales rep pitches in their proposal. Watch those channels and see who else is advertising there. Make a determination if you feel your music would be a nice fit for a given network.

When consumers who don't care about what you're selling see your commercial, you're only wasting your money. If you're a rock group or a rap artist, advertising on a channel that airs old B&W movies or arts and crafts shows targeted for the elderly will not be helping you sell CDs or increase attendance at concerts. For the majority of my clients, I suggest they run their commercials on MTV, VH1, FUSE and BET.

And let's be honest, getting your image, message and music on TV is very impressive to consumers. If someone sees you on MTV one evening, they might not even realize that it's only in that particular market and the surrounding suburbs. (For example, Boston and the smaller towns surrounding it.) They may think, "Wow, this artist is really big! They run commercials on MTV!" Little did they know that you only spent $50 or $60 dollars to air that spot. Ah, image!

If you are fortunate enough to have retail distribution for your record, let your distributor know that you are planning to run commercials. (If this is something you decide to do one day.) Sometimes, distributors will go to retail chains and ask them to purchase a large amount of CDs, in return you would plug, or "tag" their stores in the commercial. The commercial would also feature the retail chain's logo and even the name mentioned in the voiceover.

It's a very simple proposition. If they will carry your CDs in their stores, you will mention them in your commercials and attempt to drive consumers in to make a purchase. The best part for the store is that you're not asking them for any money towards the slots.

For example, towards the end of the commercial, the record store's logo would appear on the screen and the voiceover artist mentions something like "Buy this CD exclusively at Timothy's Records, throughout New Jersey." I'm sure you've seen this a million times at the end of commercials.

When a retail chain sees an artist or a label spending money on print ads, radio spots and television commercials, they realize they are dealing with serious professionals. It makes it a lot easier for them to say yes when you approach them to carry your CDs and merchandise. (Especially if you are willing to tag your ads, spots and commercial with their name and/or logo.)

ADDITIONAL TIPS

When a client sends me the rough draft of their commercial for my feedback, I watch it a few times. Then I watch it with the mute button engaged to see if a viewer would still be able to understand what the artist and the product was all about. I then watch it a few more times with the voice turned back on. I want to see if I continue to enjoy the presentation, or if it's beginning to bore me.

TOURING

Live performances are an important part of building a buzz. You should perform at least eight times per month, if at all possible. Performing enables you to win over new fans, sell a number of records and build up your mailing list.

It allows writers from local newspapers and regional publications to see you "in action." You can also earn money from the club owner or booking agency if you build up a loyal following and regularly get people out to see you. The more you play, the better chance you will have of receiving higher pay, while getting gigs in the bigger establishments around your region.

As you climb the ladder of success, you will want to continue to tour. Touring is not just for new artists. You will want to keep your name and music in the minds of the record buying public. Being on the road, along with all of the supplemental promotion, marketing and publicity keep the artist visible and popular.

Some artists make the mistake of putting their career in cruise control once they start tasting some success. Don't make that mistake. If you are fortunate enough to "make it" you must continue to work hard to stay at the top. Fans and the media can be very fickle and quickly switch their allegiance to another artist, if you are not out there promoting and marketing yourself regularly. Touring is among the best ways to stay on their minds and in their hearts. In the concert setting, the fan is right in the room with you and that personal bond can be very strong and lasting.

Record companies realize the importance of touring, in relation to building and maintaining a buzz and increasing record sales. If they are scouting a new artist and see that touring is already a part of their regimen, it will certainly give them brownie points, when being compared to another artist who does not tour or perform on a regular basis. In addition to clubs, consider other venues to perform at. Colleges, outdoor festivals, cafes and various charity events are often great opportunities for a new artist looking for new places to perform.

Don't always be so concerned with what you're being paid for the performance. Of course, you should try to get what is fair. But, remember, your main goal in the early stages of your career is to use the opportunity as a way to gain some experience and win over new fans. Selling CDs and merchandise is a nice plus as well of course!

At every gig, you should announce that you have a mailing list. After your performance, pass around a pad and pen so that people can sign up if they are interested in your act. Every month or so, mail postcards or send e-mail that announce upcoming gigs and provide fans with additional news and information. This is a great way to keep fans posted on what is happening with your project.

As your mailing list begins to grow, you can exchange it with other acts that have similar styles. Most artists are doing all of this via e-mail, while some still mail postcards or form letters to the fans on their list. Exchanging list with others can virtually double each of your respective mailing lists overnight. In return, you'll gain new fans, sell CDs and get more people out to your upcoming live performances.

I know that sounds obvious to some of you, but I see so many people that don't bother to even try to collect names and e-mail addresses for their project. I know it takes a little effort, but please, people.... Mention that you have a list and where they can walk over and sign up after your performance.

Even if you're playing one night and the crowd is small. So what? If you get ten people to sign up for your monthly updates, that's ten more than you had yesterday. Do that a few times and watch the size of your list grow.

Touring is an essential part of the music business for a majority of recording artists. New artists look at the road as an exciting way to see the country, make new fans, perform their music and make a comfortable living. These ideals may seem wonderful, but being on the road is hard work. Most artists find that as long as they are making music, touring isn't so bad after all. Touring is especially necessary for new artists who are trying to build a fan base. Artists need to keep their name fresh in the mind of the public. Videos are certainly a great promotional tool, but never underestimate the importance of performing live.

Tours will generally increase record sales in the markets where you are performing. Performing on the road can also be a source of added income. As your following grows and you begin to play the larger venues, your pay should also begin to increase. Many established artists often make more money from arena-level world tours and merchandise than they ever do from record sales. You must prepare a budget before you officially book the tour. You will have to determine how much the tour will cost you, especially if you don't have a label advancing tour support monies.

There are dozens of things to take into consideration. Sample expenditures would include the cost of ground and air transportation, hotels, meals, gas, tolls, road crew salaries, equipment and any other miscellaneous expenses that may arise.

After all of that information is collected, calculate what each venue is paying you for the show. In some cases, the expenses may be larger than the income from your performances. You'll probably be able to sell CDs and merchandise, but set realistic goals as you prepare your budget. Many unsigned or small independent artists feel fortunate to sell $200 worth of CDs and merchandise after each show. I know some acts that sell far more than that after each gig. You will have to make your own realistic sales projections.

T-shirts can be designed and manufactured for under three dollars each when bought in large quantities. You can sell those on the road for ten dollars and make a tidy profit. The additional income will help to supplement your tour budget. Because odds are, you're won't be getting paid a ton of money for those early road trips. Other merchandise items such as key chains, posters and baseball-style caps are also inexpensive ways to promote your act while bringing in additional income.

Most club patrons are going to spend their money on drinks. They would rather buy an extra beer or two instead of an unknown artist's CD. Take that into consideration as you plan your CD and merchandise income projections.

Before you even consider planning and booking a tour, you must do your homework and prepare diligently. You must be able to put on a show that is entertaining and professional. The band and the crew must be well rehearsed and capable of successfully handling their respective responsibilities night after night.

Song selection, equipment set up and breakdown, sound technicians, lights, wardrobe, choreography, security, hotels and transportation must be organized before the tour can actually begin. All of the flaws must be worked out in rehearsal, and the entire production must be a solid, cohesive unit. This includes the act, the personal manager, the road manager and the entire crew. Everyone has to be on the same page and fully aware of their duties and obligations.

The road crew must know how to load, unload, and set up all of the equipment in an efficient and fast manner. Some venues only give the opening act a few minutes to pull this off. The sound and lights people have to understand their jobs and coordinate their efforts so the performance sounds and looks as great as possible. Merchandisers and mailing list organizers must be ready to roll as well. You must run everything like a well oiled machine.

Always remember to travel with some small flashlights. Once the lights go down in a concert venue, it gets very dark and you may need to see things that you are working on, such as the equipment, a set list or the sound board. You'll be glad that you have the flashlight with you.

Make sure that whatever is needed for traveling is confirmed well enough in advance. You don't want to roll into Cleveland at midnight after a seven hundred mile drive and find out there is a big convention in town, and all of the hotel rooms are booked solid. Sleeping in a van in the winter in most states is a frozen nightmare. You should also have maps and good directions to each venue, radio station, record store and hotel.

Your manager, or someone in the act, should have sent a CD, poster and press kit to each of the clubs on your itinerary four or five weeks before the show. This will help to advertise your upcoming appearance. You should also bring a decent amount of promotional materials on the road. You'll be able to give out CDs and press kits if you happen to meet any music industry professionals, such as radio personnel, members of the print media and promoters.

It is also advisable to be prepared for any potential emergencies. Your road manager should have certain personal information on each artist and crew member in case of an accident or illness. They should have everyone's name, address, emergency contact phone numbers, social security number, and information on any medical conditions, allergies or prescription drugs that a physician might need to be made aware of in an emergency situation. It is also important to have information on everyone's health insurance carrier, in case it is necessary to contact them. If traveling outside of the country, be sure to have a valid passport.

It's also wise to bring a copy of the contracts between the artist and the various venues along with you on the tour. Be sure that your personal manager or a member of your team also has a copy of these contracts at home, as a back up. In case any disputes arise regarding what you are supposed to be paid, or what is on your rider, it's best to have the written contract available right at the moment of the dispute.

I've heard too many stories where the artist did not have a copy of the contract and rider with them on the road. Then when a problem with a venue manager occurred, they had no written proof of their agreement. If your contract calls for $500 in guaranteed pay and at the end of the night the venue gives you $150 – you better have the paperwork in your hands, not hundreds of miles away back at home. If you are fortunate enough to have a road manager, he or she has to do their best to keep things running smoothly during the tour. The artist should be shielded from petty problems and allowed to remain focused on performing. Someone with experience can be a tremendous asset to an artist.

Professional Road Managers, (RM) usually have music industry contacts in every major city. They also have the ability to properly deal with problems that occur during a tour, such as travel delays and equipment failure. If you are an unsigned band and your advisors are able to put together a small regional tour, you should strongly consider finding a road manager.

A day in the life of a RM is very busy and often filled with making important decisions on the spot. Their first job is to make sure the artist, the traveling party and the equipment make it safely and successfully from city to city along the tour route. If there is a problem with any of the people, the gear or the vehicle, the road manager must solve those dilemmas in a hurry.

During load in at the venue, the RM must keep an eye on things as the equipment is being set up and during the sound check. The RM is really like an extension of the Personal Manager, when the (PM) cannot attend a show or shows.

If the artist and traveling party head back to the bus or a hotel for a meal and a nap after sound check, the RM must make sure that there is security present to guard the equipment at the venue, until, during and after the performance. Before the gig, the RM should also check the dressing room to make sure it is clean, comfortable and that it contains the food, beverages and other items that were agreed to in the contract.

The RM also looks after the artist and makes sure they get to any other place they must visit during their stay in a give town, such as a radio station or record store. During the actual show, a pro RM will keep on the move to make sure the sound and light people are doing their jobs correctly. The RM will also periodically check in on the merchandise tables and backstage area.

At the end of the concert, the RM usually meets with the concert promoter or venue manager to get an accounting of ticket sales and pick up the artist's pay for that particular concert. Most venues will pay by check these days. But if a few pay by cash, make arrangements to get that money deposited as quickly as possible. If someone breaks into your van, bus or hotel room, you don't want them making off with thousands of dollars of your hard earned cash. I've heard of artists keeping $50,000 or more in a box on their tour bus. I don't think that's a good idea at all.

Since the RM is an extension of the PM on the road, as I mentioned earlier, I always suggest that the RM provide the PM with a written assessment after each show. This can be done via e-mail or fax. It's crucial that the PM is kept abreast of everything!

Topics of this formal assessment would include the quality of the artist's performance, the efforts of the crew, including sound and lights, the audience's reaction to the show, especially if a few new songs were performed, how much merchandise was sold, the number of people who joined the mailing list and if the promoter or venue honored the terms of the rider. The document can be wrapped up with an update on how much money the artist received after the show and the manner in which the artist was paid, be it cash or a check.

The PM will greatly appreciate this and the artist should encourage the RM to do this after each and every show. At the conclusion of the tour, the PM and the artist should review the written reports, along with information from the record company and/or distributor showing CD sales in each market of the tour. It will be important to analyze what impact a concert had in relation to retails sales in each market in the days and weeks after the tour rolled through each town. The goal here should be to see impressive spikes in sales in each market in the days and weeks after the concert.

Another thing that seems so obvious, but so few people remember to do it after a tour, is to send a thank you card or note to anyone and everyone that helped along the way while out on the road. This list should include your manager, booking agent, attorney, road crew, security, promoters, venue managers, publicist, record company, radio stations, press and so on. People will be working very hard behind the scenes to make your tour a success. Make sure you take some time to say thanks. This simple gesture of kindness will go a long way.

There are negative aspects to touring that you should be aware of as well. Keep in mind that you may actually lose money after all of your expenses are deducted from any income. You will also be sacrificing home-cooked meals and a proper amount of sleep. Touring artists live out of a suitcase for months at a time, and the constant travel is quite grueling.

Often, people attending concerts are rude towards the opening act because they are there to see the headliner. You will have to deal with people screaming at you to end your set so the other artist can take the stage. Touring is not as glamorous as one might think, but the benefits far outweigh the drawbacks in the eyes of most people. Just do your best and hopefully you will win over some of the people in the audience and make new fans.

As a new act, you must remember that the main goal of touring cannot be money. You'll only be disappointed if that's the case. The reason that you are touring is to promote your career and sell CDs. Use the opportunity to win over many new fans, which in turn will heighten your buzz. You will also have the opportunity to establish yourself as a regional or national act. Most artists do not want to play at the corner tavern or local community center for the rest of their careers. They want their music to reach a larger audience.

Opening act status may not be the most prestigious role, but it may be a stepping stone for bigger and better things down the road. Maybe someday you will be the headlining act. Remain focused on the real objectives of touring and you won't be let down. Cities all start to look the same, and you don't see your family and friends for long periods of time. Being on the road can also put a tremendous strain on relationships. However, you must be aware of the commitment and sacrifices you have to make if you are going to be a success in the music business.

Many curious musicians wonder what a typical day on the road is like. Most days start off with an early morning radio station interview and then a stop at a local record store for a promotional in-store appearance. From there it's time to grab a cell phone and do some phone interviews with the print media and radio stations in the cities that you are about to hit on the tour.

After an afternoon load-in and sound check, the artist usually goes back to the hotel or bus to take a nap and have dinner. Then comes the best part of the day, the performance! Then it's back on the bus for an overnight drive to the next city where the entire process is repeated again. You have to realize that touring is a great deal more than just performing. The other twenty-three hours in the day are filled with travel and promotional obligations.

Do your best to get as much rest of possible. Between the afternoon naps in the hotel and the sleep during the overnight drives, utilize that down time to get rest. Try to eat healthy and drink plenty of water while on the road. These days, many hotels have exercise equipment and swimming pools. Use these as opportunities to stay in shape. If you partake in any romantic encounters on the road, make sure you're smart and take the necessary precautions. It could save your life.

Remember, you are on the road to promote your music and sell CDs and merchandise. Being on tour is not a license to act like a fool getting loaded every night and sleeping with someone new seven days a week. If you worked a 9 to 5 job at a big corporation you wouldn't act like that. Because if you did, you'd be fired before you even sobered up! Take your career seriously or it won't be a career for very long.

I've been asked many times what a Tour Rider looks like for an established artist who's touring at the theatre or arena level. So I decided to add one to this chapter for your reading pleasure. This is a sample rider that I use as a starting template when a client needs one drafted for an upcoming tour.

The numbers can be adjusted, based on the size of the touring party. I know most unsigned acts are happy with some water, beer and pretzels, but check out how the other half lives...

SAMPLE TOUR RIDER

48 - 1.5 liter bottles Water in a bucket of clean ice

12 bottles of assorted Gatorade

2 six-packs of Coca-Cola

2 six-packs of Pepsi

2 six-packs of Coors Light Beer

2 six-packs of Budweiser Beer

1 bottle of premium red wine

4 cheese pizzas

1 deli tray to serve 12 people

1 veggie platter with dip

1 large fresh-fruit tray

1 loaf of white bread

1 large bowl of pretzels

1 large coffee maker with skim milk, sugar, stirrers & cups

12 cotton bath towels

If you are signed to a label when you are getting ready to tour, make sure they know your entire itinerary the moment dates have been confirmed. This will give the people in promotion, marketing and publicity time to formulate their plan of attack and start implementing it.

Be sure that your distributor is also aware of your tour dates. That way they have the time to get CDs into the stores in the markets where you will be performing. Someone on your team must send promotional posters to each venue, so they can be placed on the wall long before your arrival.

About two weeks before you arrive in a market, you should have someone from your team calling record stores there, to make sure records are in the stores. If CDs are not on the shelves, you or your manager should call the label or distributor immediately and let them know. I've heard of too many indie label artists busting their tails on the road, only to have someone forget to make sure records were in the stores in a market (or markets) during a tour. So immediately after successful publicity, marketing, radio promotion and a gig, they didn't capture one retail sale because the next morning the consumer couldn't find the record!

Do you want to guess what happens then? The consumer spends their money on someone else's CD and you're left out in the cold. Don't let that scenario happen to you. Make sure record stores have your record in stock before you roll into town.

If you're all over Boston radio and the darling of their print media and your gig sold out in two days – that's great! But if there are no CDs in the stores in Boston, (or there's only five copies) – then you or someone really dropped the ball. Most labels and distributors represent a great deal of artists and sometimes they can't do everything. Don't put your complete trust in anyone. Look out for your own best interests and make a few calls to key record stores in each city of your tour.

There is so much competition for the entertainment dollar. You simply must capture those retail sales when you can. There is no excuse for failure in this area. Billboard has a great guide that lists all of the retail record stores.

When the time is right in your career, buy that book and use it often!

Another thing that drives me crazy is when people plan and route tours in a haphazard manner. I read tour itineraries on a regular basis and the majority are well planned and thought out. But every few months someone sends me their tour schedule and I scratch my head in complete disbelief. A Tuesday in Minneapolis, followed by a Wednesday in Philadelphia, then a Thursday in Chicago and Friday in Baltimore! I understand that venues are busy with other events and every tour can't be routed perfectly, but please try to organize your tours in a logical manner. Especially with gas price these days!

I would also like to stress the importance of insurance for your musical equipment. I have heard sad stories from countless recording artists through the years who have had gear stolen while on the road. Believe me, I feel sorry for those people. But since your livelihood is earned with those instruments, please invest in some insurance to protect it.

I was once told a story about an artist who lost two prized guitars thanks to someone with no conscience. As one roadie brought gear from the stage out to the sidewalk, the other crew member would take it from the curb and place it in the van. In a matter of two minutes while Roadie #1 was in the van arranging gear, Roadie #2 placed the expensive guitars near the street and ran back in for the next load. By the time Roadie #1 stepped back outside to grab the guitars, they were gone.

Since the group had no insurance on their equipment and very little cash in their pockets, they bought some no name beginner's guitar for $150 and finished the tour with that instrument. Again, don't let this happen to you. Get a few price quotes on insurance and sign up. In the terrible event that something like that happens to you, at least you could get some money back to buy new gear.

Listen, I'm not here to tell anyone how to live their personal life. But I will warn you about traveling on tour with illegal substances in your possession. Don't be foolish enough to do this. Ever.

First of all, if you get pulled over for speeding, with out-of-state license plates no less, and the state police officer sees that it's a traveling music group, there's a fairly good chance you may get searched. Stereotypes are not fair, but some people still give those weight as they make decisions. This will especially be the case if they smell marijuana or see empty beer or liquor bottles in the vehicle. If you get arrested for driving while under the influence of alcohol or possession of illegal drugs 500 miles from home, at 2:00 in the morning, you're in big trouble. By the time you find an attorney and straighten out that mess, you probably will have missed at least one gig. If it's a weekend or a holiday and a judge is not around, you'll most likely miss more than one show!

I'm sure you can guess that if you miss a performance for a reason as stupid as the one in this scenario, you're going to have a long line of angry people to deal with. Including, but not limited to the venue, your manager, booking agent, lawyer, distributor and most importantly, your fans.

I remember hearing a story about a rock group getting pulled over in the mid 90's. The officer could smell beer on the driver's breath and the odor of marijuana was apparently quite strong too. He made everyone get out of the vehicle and stand on the side of the highway. Some of the members were sleeping in the back of the RV and stumbled outside in shorts and T-shirts. It was not July or August by the way, it was cold and windy. They were asked to open all of their luggage and road cases. There they were, unpacking their belongings, with cars flying by at seventy miles per hour, half asleep, on the side of some highway.

Unfortunately for them, they did indeed have some illegal substances in their possession, and their next stop was downtown. Between fines, attorney fees and loss of gigs, their little "party" cost them over four thousand dollars. Ouch!

Remember that this is your career. Grow up and leave your bad habits behind. People are becoming much less tolerant of this sort of behavior, especially in the music and entertainment fields. It's not cool or cute anymore. Serious industry pros are out to make money and preserve their integrity and honorable reputation. If you're a fool, you'll find it quite a challenge to get any big shots to work with you. Trust me on this one.

I remember attending a label showcase a few years ago for a client. The singer was amazing, but clearly, he partied a little too hard that evening. During the last song of the set, he strolled off stage and was just staring at his bandmates. He looked at me and commented what a great group was on stage. The scary part is, he didn't realize it was HIS group. The guitar player just kept soloing while looking around for the singer. I told him to get back on the stage to finish the song! Don't ever make this mistake in your career. If you want to have a few drinks after a show, that's your business. Just don't let it interfere with your performance or let down your colleagues.

Another question that I get asked at least a few times each month involves opening act opportunities for unsigned artists. It's usually asked by acts that have sold three or four dozen CDs and have a whopping five or six college radio stations spinning their record. They call and say they just read about some superstar act who's about to launch a tour and how can they become the opening act. Do you see the folly in this question yet?

First of all, the music business is all about "who you know." So if you don't have a well connected and respected manager and booking agent, and you've only sold 200 CDs, it's a safe bet to assume you won't be playing Madison Square Garden later this month.

Opening acts for hot tours are often chosen through a complex formula that includes strong sales at retail, success at radio, television and with the print media and those with a powerful buzz throughout the industry. Having well connected representation is also crucial. A powerful label behind you is always a nice plus too!

Some superstar acts reportedly even charge a fee to an opening act for the opportunity to be on the tour. Established artists realize the value in allowing a new act to perform in front of twenty-thousand people each and every night during a national or international tour. This is an amazing amount of exposure and they realize what's being put on the table for the emerging artist.

It's a great opportunity for you to sell records, merchandise and expand your fan base. That being the case, some people want a fee in exchange for an opening slot. Since this figure may be in the five to six figure range, you better have a supportive label willing to pay the piper! This is often referred to as a "buy-on."

Additional Tips

Be prepared when you are about to begin performing live. Know your songs inside and out. Rehearse over and over. Put together a show that has a smooth flow to it. Act professional if problems with equipment or the monitors happen during a set. Don't let malfunctions with gear or an intoxicated heckler ruin your performance. Speaking of intoxication – please act like a professional. There's no need to be on stage under the influence of alcohol or drugs, or with a cigarette hanging out of your mouth. And let's keep the banter between the songs to a PG rating. No one wants to hear you spewing a few dozen f-bombs. Really, it's not cool.

In your rehearsals, you should practice what you want to say in between songs. Be sure and mention the artist's name three to five times during the set. Plug the CD, let people know where it's available. Let the fans know your Web site address. Introduce each song by stating the title. Encourage people to join your mailing list. All they have to do is write down their e-mail address on your clipboard or pad after the show. Make sure you purchase a nice banner to hang in the back of the stage, during each show. Use a font or logo this is easy to read, even from a distance and when lighting is not favorable.

If the venue gives you a forty-five minute set, don't play for one minute longer. Other artists have to take the stage and if even one group plays an extra song or two, it throws off the whole evening. Have some consideration. Do your thing and get off the stage. Once your set is over, I always encourage an artist to promptly get their gear out of the way so the next act can begin setting up. Once everything is packed and stored safely, then it's time to mingle with the crowd, sell CDs and merchandise and get people to sign up for your mailing list. You are there to work and to promote your music. Have drinks, chat with your buddies or shoot pool some other time.

If you regularly do all of these things, then great! I applaud your professionalism. If you are not carefully following this advice at each gig, then make a mental note to start addressing these issues at your very next show.

RECORD COMPANIES

There are thousands of record companies in the United States. Some are considered "Major Labels" (Majors) and others are considered "Independent Labels" (Indies). It's important for you to have a general understanding about each of these companies. There are similarities and differences between both that you should be aware of.

The music industry is in the midst of a profound transition. New distribution mechanisms are shifting power to independent labels. These trends are resulting in a wider selection of genres and artists, requiring a focus on smaller, more specific target markets. For major labels, addressing these changes is clearly at odds with their old school mass marketing business models. While demand for a wider and more diverse selection of artists increases, majors are actually reducing their rosters to concentrate on the most successful acts. At the same time, the distribution networks that once represented the largest barriers to reaching niche segments across the country are being wiped out by emerging technologies and secure digital downloads.

These factors have lead industry analysts to predict dramatic changes in how consumers discover new artists, spend their money on recorded music and who benefits from this profound shift in power. Long standing marketing and distribution models are being eroded more and more each year. The climate is certainly right for independent labels to prosper and grow to heights people would not have even imagined a decade ago.

Most record companies are divided into a number of departments, each handling various responsibilities and duties. While not every company is fashioned in the same manner, the following is a basic outline that can help you better understand most of the various departments.

The Artists & Repertoire (A&R) Department's responsibilities include discovering new talent, choosing songs for acts on their roster, and finding the right producer and recording studio for their respective projects. They also act as the artist's intermediary between the other departments of the record company. The A&R Department is the creative force behind the label. By the way, some A&R executives are also record producers.

The Promotion Department is responsible for getting the records played on radio stations. Most of the larger record companies have regional promotional people that concentrate on certain markets. Radio airplay is carefully tracked and reported to the other departments of the record company for analysis.

Sales & Marketing Departments are concerned with getting records into the retail stores, print advertising and media buying campaigns and record store displays. They work very hard to create and implement a successful marketing plan that is coordinated with people in the other departments. These executives place advertisements in music magazines and coordinate radio & television commercials when a new record is about to be released.

They also concentrate on getting the artist favorable press coverage through interviews, promotional appearances, and press conferences. This is one of the most important departments that a signed artist will deal with. An effective publicity and marketing campaign is vital if the artist is every going to sell a great deal of records. Be very polite and thankful to the people in this department. Many labels have Sales and Marketing divided into two separate departments. Regardless of the name and structure, be appreciative to everyone at the label, especially in the key departments handling promotion, publicity, marketing and sales. Try to remain a priority with those executives.

The Business and Legal Affairs Departments provide legal counsel for the record company. They draft contracts, licenses and other legal documents. Contract negotiating and other important business related matters are also controlled by these departments.

Accounting Departments oversee the computation of royalty checks and handle other financial related matters. These departments also maintain the record company's "bottom line" by keeping track of income and expenditures. Some labels call this their Finance Department.

INDEPENDENT LABELS

Many independent labels find success by focusing on a certain style of music such as jazz, dance or children's music. They will only sign and develop artists that they feel have potential in their particular niche market. These labels know the ins and outs of promoting and marketing the acts on their roster.

Many of these indies are capable of moving tens of thousands of units for their acts. The bigger independent labels have national distribution deals as an outlet for getting their CDs into retail stores across the country. In many cases, they also have various territorial distribution deals in foreign countries as well.

The more successful indies have the financial ability to record, manufacture, promote, market and distribute an artist in a professional and efficient manner.

Another important advantage of indie labels is their roster size. Most indies have a limited number of acts on their roster. This allows the promotion and marketing departments the luxury of doing their jobs more thoroughly. You are sometimes better off being one of five artists on a roster, rather than one of ninety! You generally have the opportunity to receive more attention if you are a part of a smaller label. It's not as easy to get lost in the shuffle at a smaller record company, compared to a larger operation.

Many of the indie labels will take the time to help with properly developing an artist. They often take the grass-roots method of building up a loyal following. Many count on their acts to tour relentlessly.

College radio stations are another source that small and mid-sized labels turn to for promotion when they are trying to break a new act. Quite often, major commercial radio stations will not play independent label releases, unless a record really starts to take off. I would define "take off" as the record is ruling the college radio airwaves, the artist is getting a ton of favorable press in national magazines and large market newspapers, their tour is a big success and the CD is selling extremely well at retail.

Don't underestimate the importance of college radio. First of all, in the early days, they may be the only radio outlet that you will have at your disposal. Secondly, if you can climb the charts on stations that report their playlist to C.M.J. (College Music Journal) – then you have an opportunity to be noticed by the print media, retail and larger record companies. Many industry executives keep a close eye on the C.M.J. charts to see what unsigned or indie artists are making noise on the airwaves. Some of the larger record companies have research departments that spend many hours each week searching for artists who are doing well on the indie circuit.

Independent labels are not known for giving the large advances that the majors are synonymous for. There are also times when little or no advance is given, but the record company picks up the cost of recording, manufacturing and promotion. It is important for your manager and lawyer to negotiate to get you the best deal possible.

"Best deal" should not be translated into "most advance money." An experienced entertainment lawyer will know what to negotiate for, in addition to money, so your contract will be as favorable to you as possible. Creative control, a fair royalty rate, a serious commitment to the promotional and touring campaigns and a guaranteed release date are also very important issues that should be addressed.

There are many independent record companies out there. If your music and live show are great and you are creating a solid buzz, you may be able to attract the attention of someone. Indies are often a great way for an act to get to that elusive "next level," but those smaller labels also have some disadvantages and limitations that should be looked at with careful consideration and with realistic expectations.

If you are fortunate enough to secure a deal with an indie, you cannot just sit back and count on the label's resources and efforts to carry you. Your work is just beginning once you sign on the dotted line. You have to work harder than ever to supplement what the label does for you. You should coordinate your efforts with the label at all times. Considerate it a team effort and don't think that they will do everything and you can simply show up at your gigs and play for forty-five minutes. Your efforts will be 24/7, not just for the length of your live set. This level of commitment really goes for an indie or a major deal. You have to capitalize on that opportunity before you lose it.

Make sure that your personal manager and the label are on the same page when it comes to promotion, marketing and distribution. You do not want them driving your career in several different directions at once. The label, the personal manager and the artist must have a clearly defined plan before a new release hits the stores. Everyone's vision must be the same.

This sounds obvious, but you wouldn't believe how many times things are done in an inefficient manner because people have their own agenda, rather than being a team player. Ultimately, it's the artist whose career pays the price if things are done incorrectly. This sort of problem can also occur with major labels, so don't let your guard down in that case either.

Another disadvantage of independent record companies is that they often have poor distribution, while others have none at all. Retail distribution is something that you must inquire about. The promotion, publicity and touring may be going great, but if consumers cannot find your CD in their local store, you will not be fully capitalizing on your success.

Some indie labels have a very small staff. There are only so many hours in the day, and if the same person is running A&R, marketing, promotion, sales and the accounting departments, chances are that some things are not being done to peak efficiency. Guess who pays the price in the long run?

Regardless of what size label that you may be on someday, be sure that you and your personal manager know people in each of the various departments. These relationships are very important. The lines of communication have to be working properly to successfully get the project off the ground. If the promotional staff members are not enthusiastic about your music, it can be a huge problem.

If your manager yelled at a label staffer for no good reason and got them into trouble with their supervisor, don't think that their heart will be into pushing your music. Don't let a big ego or an ungrateful attitude tarnish your name at the record company. Remember to be polite and thank people for a job well done. Many artists forget to do that. Everyone enjoys hearing the words "Thank You" after a job well done.

I've always been a firm believer that you get more from people with honey than vinegar. So if you expect people to work hard on your behalf, be nice, be polite and be gracious. Check the ego at the door when dealing with people in this industry. Especially with people that have the ability to help, or hurt, your career!

BUSINESS SITUATION (SWOT) ANALYSIS
Now let's take a deep look into a hypothetical independent record company, to see, on average, the typical strengths,

weaknesses, opportunities and threats facing their operation. While each bullet point does not apply to every label, it will give you a good idea as to the inner workings of a new independent label about to embark on their mission.

INTERNAL
- Strengths
- Weaknesses

EXTERNAL
- Opportunities
- Threats

STRENGTHS
- Experienced and dedicated executive team and outside consultants.

- The resources and knowledge to capitalize on emerging technology.

- Excellent talent scouts (Artists & Repertoire) and recording artists.

- Years of industry experience have earned the executives strong contacts in the print media and with radio stations across the country.

- Outstanding Internet and retail distribution capabilities.

- A state-of-the art computer system, Web site & e-commerce system, that utilizes the latest technology to enhance productivity and efficiency.

- A staff that is passionate about the music and its work.

- Serious commitment to customer service and customer retention.

WEAKNESSES
- New brand name without much recognition with consumers & the media.

- Limited financial resources.

- Dependent on narrow streams of income, generally CD & merchandise sales.

- Internet business model for marketing & distribution in the music industry is new and untested.

- Limited number of employees.

OPPORTUNITIES
- Opportunities to become the e-distribution source for smaller, niche market record companies.

- A large number of former major label artists who are now "independent" and looking for a new record company to partner with.

- Rapid Internet growth is compelling companies to market music worldwide.

- Growth that is occurring in the musical genres that the Company specializes in.

- The large number of retail record stores closing down, forcing consumers to purchase music via the Internet or mail order.

THREATS
- The music industry is still vulnerable to consumers who choose to illegally download music.

- Larger, established record companies are recognizing niches and beginning to compete aggressively in areas once ignored.

- The merging and consolidation of the major record labels and the threat of a potential monopoly situation in the music industry.

- With the affordability of recording, compact disc production and digital distribution, more artists are having the opportunity to record and release music without a record company's involvement or support.

- A negative change in the U.S. economy may force consumers to curb their spending on entertainment and related products.

- A bad review in a major, national magazine can harm CDs sales and an artist's rising popularity.

RISKS
- Willingness of consumers to discover and research new music via the Internet.

- Willingness of consumers to purchase music within a digital environment.

- Protection and enforcement of intellectual property and copyright laws.

- Limited financial resources of most new independent labels.

CUSTOMER ACQUISITION
Since many people reading this book own or plan to launch their own independent record company, I wanted to briefly touch upon the relationship between businesses and their customers. The cost of customer acquisition must be important to all indie labels. This figure is based upon the total cost of advertising and marketing expenditures, divided by the number of new customers secured during a given campaign. The best way for the label to recoup these expenses is by not only acquiring new customers, but by retaining those people for many years to come. You must view anyone who is purchasing your music, merchandise and concert tickets as your "customer."

Labels must work hard to build relationships with their "customers" in an effort to increase the probability that those people will return for purchases on a regular basis. The importance of brand loyalty cannot be ignored. I'm sure many people reading this book could easily name a few record companies that they love and often purchase anything released by those labels. If a label is successful, a number of loyal consumers will get to a point where they trust and embrace everything put out by that company.

An independent record company must strive to be viewed the first choice for consumers, content providers, advertising partners and business partners as the company that consistently releases great music, is among the easiest to work with and is able to form synergistic strategic alliances better than any other entity in the music industry. Online and offline advertising have to be paired with traditional promotional campaigns to reach out, secure and keep new customers in a successful and efficient manner. The label's ultimate goal should be to not only meet, but exceed the customer's expectations throughout the entire marketing and sales process.

To acquire new customers, labels should rely on several key methods, including, but not limited to:

- Advertising (Traditional & Internet)

- Direct Marketing (Traditional & Internet)

- An amazing Web site and aggressive campaigns driving consumers to the site

- Radio Promotion

- Publicity

- Print Ads

- Television & Radio Commercials

- Concert Tours

- Music Videos

- Strategic alliances with other appropriate companies

- Trade Shows/Music Conferences/Festivals

CUSTOMER RETENTION

In their effort to retain customers, labels should use personal, friendly e-mail communications to everyone on their master customer list, on a monthly basis. They must look at these relationships with a long-term focus. Make free song samples, tour dates, artist news, contests and exclusive interviews available to established customers first. Try to foster a friendly, trustworthy approach, so fans of your operation feel like their standing entitles them to a variety of benefits long before "the general public" would see or hear it.

Never make the common mistake of overlooking the value of existing customer relationships, as you pursue new ones. You must realize that if customers feel ignored and unimportant, they will eventually take their business to another company who also provides high quality music. Customer satisfaction is important to gaining more customers and keeping the ones you have already secured. Some of these rules will apply if you are an indie label, or if you have formed one solely as a vehicle for your original music.

You must retain existing customers and make sure those people make regular and steady purchases if they want to see the business remain profitable. Some industries that sell merchandise with a high profit margin may not put a large focus on customer retention. But in the music industry, you do not have that luxury. You must design and implement cost effective ways to market existing customers and keep those fans loyal.

I always encourage labels to train their employees to ensure every customer walks away from a transaction satisfied and happy with their experience. If there is a problem, employees will be quickly ready to remedy it and express a sincere apology for the mishap and inconvenience. When warranted, free downloads, autographed merchandise and even prompt refunds are to be made available — so customers can see the commitment to a positive shopping experience. The competitive advantage successful customer service provides can never be underestimated.

COMMON DIFFERENCES BETWEEN
A SUCCESSFUL INDIE AND AN AVERAGE ONE

SUCCESSFUL	AVERAGE COMPETITOR
Wide variety of music from well known artists, as well as emerging/newer acts	Mostly only releases up & coming artists with a small initial following
Retail Distribution to over 5,000 stores	Regional or no retail distribution at all
Top download technology, credit card capable and in-house order fulfillment for traditional CDs	Possibly the same in most cases, except many smaller indie farm out download & traditional fulfillment to a third party
A sincere commitment to customer service and retention, with clearly defined polices and procedures	Unskilled customer service representatives, high employee turnover and difficult/confusing return policies in some cases
A Web site that is modern, entertaining, informative, easy to navigate and updated daily	Boring, "amateur looking" Web site rarely updated and complicated to navigate

If you own, or plan to start an indie label, there are several tips that I would like to give you. Our industry is clearly going through a turbulent period. Important topics such as label mergers, retail distribution changes, digital download models and emerging technologies are making for an unpredictable climate at this point in time. Being the leader of a music related business today is not easy.

Make sure that your employees and artists trust you. Be honest and keep your promises. Be fair and reasonable in your dealings with people. When people lose their sense of trust in a leader, their loyalty begins to erode and they look to other people for guidance.

Clearly communicate your plans and expectations to each

employee and artist. Without this level of concise communication, people often see changes in the company's direction as a threat to their own stability and role within the organization. As plans and circumstances change and evolve, let employees know what's going on so they can see where your vision is taking the venture. Remember that as a leader, you are now a role model to your staff and to the artist roster. You cannot let your level of performance diminish. You cannot blame someone else for your mistakes.

When you realize who the best employees are on your staff, make sure you reward them. Let them know you recognize the contributions they are making to the business. Sincere praise and meaningful rewards will keep most people happy, productive and loyal. If you don't treat people correctly, they will leave and may wind up working for your competitors.

It's quite simple actually. Be sure that your staff and your artists know where you're headed, how you plan to get there, how you plan to stay there, what you expect from them and how they fit into your vision. Add in plenty of thanks and create a pleasant working environment. These are a few steps to building your label and keeping it moving in a positive direction.

MAJOR LABELS

For decades, the majors have used their incredible advantage in distribution to more than compensate for their inefficiencies in identifying, recruiting and supporting talent. With each major label having a formal distribution arm, access to retail shelf space, air time, and every element of the marketing mix has remained their exclusive domain.

In the same way a local utility company controls what kind of electricity, consumers receive, major labels have substantially controlled what kind of music the public becomes aware of, has access to, and, ultimately, buys. Consider the impact an alternative source of energy, not requiring a line into your home would have on the power structure of the electric company. The impact of digitally downloaded music, along with online ordering, is equally threatening to the world's largest record companies. Major labels are large, global companies with substantial financial resources and extensive retail distribution. Before contacting a major label, your group of advisors should be fully assembled, and you as the artist must be ready in every way.

Make sure that your team truly believes that the time is right for your approach. It's also important to get your demo to the appropriate A&R rep. If your manager gets your rock demo to the rap A&R rep, your team will look like they didn't do their homework and your chances for success with that label will be diminished.

Major label deals are not easy to achieve, but if you are fortunate enough to be offered one, you will have excellent distribution to keep your records on the shelves. Their promotion, marketing and publicity departments are staffed by experienced and talented people who know how to successfully work a record.

Their financial resources are very helpful in keeping an act on the road, which in turn puts you in the eyes and ears of the public. The power of a major label may also open up doors for an opportunity to be a support act for an established artist touring at the arena level.

Top producers and engineers are also more likely to take an interest in a major label recording artist. Factors like distribution, money, experience and clout make major labels more appealing for many artists. Did I mention money? Promotion, touring and videos are very costly. This is especially true at the national or global levels and for a sustained period of time.

Majors can get airplay on many commercial radio stations that routinely ignore independent label artists. The resources behind major label record companies allow them to do all things on a larger scale.

The downside when dealing with major labels is that, at times, a new act can get lost among the masses. If your album is released around the same time as one of their superstar acts, the promotional department may be concentrating their efforts on promoting the big star, instead of you.

Also, major labels often want to control more of the artistic and creative aspects of a newly signed project. They like to assist the artist with the selection of a producer, a recording facility, songs, graphic design and photography. Sometimes, the label can be quite adamant in its recommendations. The record companies know that they have the experience, and it's their investment money at stake.

They want the power to make the most of the decisions in the early stages of an artist's career. Many artists have their own strong vision, and if that vision does not completely agree with the label's ideas, a conflict is sure to arise. Unfortunately, in most of these scenarios, the new artist is the one who must compromise. This could include decisions such as song selection, album cover artwork, or choosing an acceptable producer. Giving up creative control can really hurt some artists.

They may end up compromising their artistic integrity or giving in to the label's demands. This usually leads to resentment and animosity between the two parties. As an artist, you must realize that you are dealing with big business, and its related red tape. Some artists are willing to play the game and hope to have more negotiating clout with the label by the time their second record is ready to be released. (If there is a second record for that matter.) Some artists feel so strongly about creative control, they will pass on an offer that feels too smothering.

Another point that should be aware of is job turnover rates. At times, major label employees choose to move from one company to another, or get fired outright. If an A&R rep signs you to their label and then leaves the company two months later, the person taking over your account may not be as enthusiastic about your music. He or she may be more interested in the artists they signed and not you.

If the people who originally believed in your act are slowly moving on to other companies, you may feel like a stranger at your own label. It's very easy to get lost in the shuffle when dealing with a large corporation. Of course, an act can also get lost at an indie. In many cases though, their employee roster comprises the owners and a handful of loyal staffers. It seems to create a more artist friendly environment in many cases.

This personal approach usually extends to the artists signed to the label. If any record company is very interested in your act, it is important for you to get to know some of the people behind the scenes. Make sure that they are committed to their company, and that they aren't looking to leave in the near future. They may not tell you their true feelings, but at least try to find out. Talk with several label employees and ask them some questions so you can ascertain the stability and enthusiasm of their staff. You should also try to gage their excitement and eagerness to work with you.

Many managers and artists feel that an enthusiastic independent record company is not a bad option to consider if they have the infrastructure, distribution and capital to do things the right way. The relationships are often more personal and direct. In most cases, the roster is smaller so more time can be devoted to each act. Indies target specific niche audiences and know how to properly market and distribute their respective artists. This hands-on approach can be very beneficial when breaking a new artist.

It seems that the major labels sometimes follow trends. They sign acts who are similar to what is hot on the charts. Indie labels are known for staying focused on a certain genre of music, regardless of its commercial success on the charts.

But the money, power, clout, promotion and distribution of a major are great things too. Of course it's possible to start your career with an indie label and later sign with a major if your sales and buzz warrant that move. It can be a tough choice if one or more offers are presented to an artist. A great argument can be made for signing with either an indie or a major. Both have their share of pros and cons.

It usually comes down to what is right for that particular artist, considering what point they are at in their career, and what their goals are. The artist, along with their personal manager, attorney and accountant should weigh the entire situation and determine which offer is overall the best. It's not a decision that should ever be rushed. You must consider all of the options available.

Try to find a record company that is genuinely enthused about your music. If they really believe in your music, their excitement should trickle down throughout the staff members. This can only help, because you need everyone pushing to get your career off the ground.

DISTRIBUTION

Distribution is simply making your music available so consumers can purchase it. Traditional retail distributors warehouse your CDs, pitch and ship the product to retailers, collect monies and ultimately pay the label or artist, depending on the structure of the deal.

There are five main ways of distributing music. You can sell CDs at your live performances, on your Web site, in retail record stores, through online stores, such as CDBaby and via digital downloads. There are quite a few companies offering digital distribution these days.

Selling CDs at your concerts is probably the most basic form of distribution. During your set, announce that CDs and merchandise are available after the show at a table in the back of the venue. Afterwards, interested parties can approach you, purchase the record and hopefully sign up for your mailing list while they're at it.

Many artists sell CDs on their Web site. While this is a great idea – and the easier you make it for consumers to find your products the better, this method of distribution comes with some excess baggage that you must consider. You must have a banking relationship to deposit checks that come in and you may even consider setting up an account so you can accept credit card orders as well.

You will also have to dedicate some time to customer service. What I mean by "customer service" is processing and shipping orders, communicating with consumers that may have a question or problem and handling all financial transactions in a prompt, courteous and professional manner.

The third place you can distribute your music is in actual retail record stores. If you have a deal directly with a distributor or a record deal that features retail distribution, then you will already have this in place. You simply want to make sure the records are in the stores and that consumers are being driven to the stores to make a purchase. Consumers are driven by your promotion, marketing, publicity, advertising and touring campaigns.

If you do not have a traditional distribution deal at retail, you should explore a consignment arrangement with a store in each market that your record is doing well in. Many record stores have various consignment deals available for local or regional acts. Give the person in charge of consignment your press kit and CD. Let them see that you are creating a buzz and that people will want to buy your latest release. If they think that nobody will be coming in to buy it, they might not want to take up valuable shelf space. Show them that you are out there making a name for yourself. Ask the store manager if you can hang up some posters advertising your CD and any upcoming local gigs.

If they agree to carry your record, then negotiate a deal. For example, if the consumer is paying $12 per CD, perhaps the store will ask for $2 or $3 per unit and the rest would go to the artist. Keep records of how many CDs each store has in stock and how often you should call to follow up on inventory and any monies owed to you. If you have consignment deals in several stores at the same time, in cities all over the country, let me warn you, it takes a lot of time and organization to stay on top of everything. You must keep great records and be prepared to make a ton of phone calls.

I strongly feel that online distribution is a great way to get your music into the hands of consumers. In my opinion, CDBaby is the KING of online distribution. Once you join CDBaby, consumers can visit the site, hear snippets of your music, read biographical information and reviews and order a CD right then and there. They even post a link to your Web site to drive traffic directly to you!

Once a consumer places an order, CDBaby conducts the entire transaction, including processing the credit card order and ships your CD from their warehouse straight to the consumer. They handle all of the customer service and send you a check for the CDs that you sell through their site. I can't image why EVERY artist is not on CDBaby. If you're not – that's your assignment for today! Check out their site and join, now! CDBaby is very artist friendly and they do a great job.

The last method of distribution that I will discuss is digital distribution. There are many companies out there that offer this service. Basically, music is uploaded to a site and consumers can find it and make a purchase. The e-distributor sends the song via the Internet to the customer, while handling the billing process on your behalf. You receive a predetermined royalty for each sale. It's pretty much that simple.

ADDITIONAL TIPS

Don't make the mistake of ordering large amounts of CDs when you first get started. I know everyone goes into a new project with great expectations, but be realistic. If things take off, you can get a reorder in less than a week in most cases. I've heard too many horror stories about indie labels and artists who've pressed up 10,000 or more CDs at the start of a campaign, only to be stuck with a garage full of product a few months later, once the sales topped off at a few thousand units.

I feel that artists and/or labels should order a reasonable amount of CDs to cover both their immediate promotional needs and what they reasonably anticipate to sell during the initial four months after release. When warranted, you can easily phone in a reorder. But at least if sales are weak, you're not stuck with 5,000 or more CDs that you paid to have manufactured, taking up space in your garage! Again, act conservatively when it comes to the number of CDs pressed. (Especially in the early days of a new release.)

If you have retail distribution and are touring at some point, make sure to have someone on your Team call ahead a few weeks before you arrive in each market, to inquire if records are on the shelves. If units are not there, call the distributor and make sure the problem is rectified... quickly. You should also ask your distributor to set up in-store promotional appearances the afternoon of a concert in a given market. In-stores are great ways to promote the act, that evening's gig and sell CDs.

If you are an indie label with a retail distribution deal, or an artist signed directly to a distributor, I strongly encourage you to stay in close contact with them. Keep the distributor posted on your success with radio and the print media. Update them on your gigs and any other favorable results from your marketing and promotion campaign. Most distributors carry a large quantity of product. Make a big effort to remain on their radar screen often.

People often ask me about P&D deals. Pressing and Distribution deals are when a large record company pays for the manufacturing of CDs and also provides retail distribution, for a smaller label, in return for a percentage of the income generated from that alliance. In most cases, the smaller label is responsible for all promotion, marketing and publicity.

Many experts suggest proceeding with caution if a P&D deal is offered to a very small indie label. With the risks of returned CDs looming over your head, it could be a dangerous road to travel, unless you are well funded and experienced in breaking a record.

MUSIC PUBLISHING

Music Publishing is a very important topic for songwriters and recording artists. It's also a complex subject that seems to be misunderstood, and causes a great deal of uncertainty for many people. The main goal of music publishing is to find ways to earn money from a song. You may have heard people use the phrase "exploiting a song." A music publisher owns song copyrights and they control the manner in which a song is used. They also collect monies from people who perform, sell or modify the material.

Under a music publishing agreement, the publisher secures ownership of a song's copyright from the writer. The publisher collects income earned by the song and forwards a share of that money to the writer.

I strongly suggest that you take the time to read as much as you can about this topic. It's an extremely important segment of the industry that may be worth a ton of money to you someday. In the meantime, here are some of the basics that you should know immediately, even before you rush over to your local library or book store...

A hot topic revolves around copyrights and how they relate to

113

music publishing. Holding the copyright in a song gives someone the right to record, reproduce, distribute, perform, publish and eventually sell the end result to consumers. Generally, the owner of the copyright is the writer of the song, or a company that the writer assigned the copyright to at some point. Copyrights can be bought or sold, therefore transferring ownership of the song to a new person or company.

The holder of the copyright attempts to earn money from this intellectual property by granting other people the right to record the song. This formal, written permission is also known as a "license." The license allows the recipient the right to record a song and then sell it to consumers.

Some writers prefer to keep all of their publishing and attempt to "exploit" the catalog through their own efforts. I've seen a few people who were successful in this manner. But most writers who really want to get their material out there choose to work with an established and well connected music publisher. Aligning with someone who works in their role as a publisher on a full time basis is a wise move. The top music publishers have a vast network of tips, leads and opportunities that most people simply don't have access to.

When it comes to presenting great songs to famous artists, large management firms, record companies, successful producers, advertising agencies, movie studios and television networks, don't underestimate the value and importance of having an experienced music publisher on your team. They can open doors that most unsigned writers and artists could never dream of getting through.

If a publisher believes in a songwriter and makes an offer, they would want the writer to assign over the song's copyright. In return for that big move, the publisher would find ways to place and exploit the song, handle the issuance of licenses, keep track of royalties owed and then divide the income with the writer.

I shop songs to labels, managers, producers and record companies on a regular basis. I also approach TV & Film leads as well. But it took many years of networking and consistently sending outstanding material to build those relationships. The top music publishers can do the same thing, but on an even larger scale. Even if you have a hit song in your catalog, if you don't know which artists are looking for material at a given time, or have a way to quickly submit a CD, then you have no chance at placing your tunes with that artist.

The larger publishers have an administrative staff to handle all paperwork, licenses, copyrights and financial transactions. Creative executives are on staff to help develop writers, improve songwriting skills and to introduce writers to other talented individuals for co-writing opportunities. They also have a manager, sometimes referred to as the "song-plugger" who utilize their industry contacts to find out who needs songs and sends packages out to those leads promptly.

If you can secure an alliance with a reputable music publisher, you should strongly consider it. But like any other contract, if a publisher makes you an offer, have an entertainment attorney review it on your behalf. You don't want to sign away anything more than what's fair and reasonable. The most common writer/publisher division of royalties is 50/50. Keep in mind, however, that there are numerous variations in the sharing of royalties, based on factors such as the number of songwriters and publishers involved and the percentages that each of those respective parties own of the song.

Here's a few publishing related terms that I'm sure you heard of, but perhaps were not exactly sure what they mean. "Mechanical royalties" are when money is paid to the owner of a copyright for the manufacturing and distribution of records. A "mechanical license" gives someone the permission to reproduce and distribute songs on a record. The most common example would be when a record company pays a royalty to an owner of a song that the label released commercially. Once the mechanical license is issued, the publisher will receive royalties as they become due.

Most mechanical licenses are negotiated through The Harry Fox Agency. Mechanical license fees are paid to HFA and after taking a small fee for administration services, the remaining monies are sent to the copyright owner, which is generally a music publisher, every three months.

Once a song is recorded and distributed to the public, the publisher must grant a license to any party who wants to cover the song. This is called a "compulsory mechanical license." Certain criteria must be met, details which are far beyond the scope of this book, which will allow someone to seek and secure a compulsory license.

If a person wishes to record a song and they file the correct paperwork and then pay a predetermined fee per record sold, this fee is known as the "statutory rate." The statutory rate slightly increases every few years and is determined by Copyright Royalty Tribunal.

When a song is performed publicly, including on television and radio, in restaurants, hotels and bars and in concert venues, the performing rights organizations monitor these events. They make license arrangements and money is collected from the user. A portion is later paid to the publisher from one of the three performing rights societies, which are BMI (Broadcast Music, Inc.), ASCAP (American Society of Composers, Authors and Publishers), and SESAC (Society of European Stage Authors and Composers). This is known as "performance royalties." The copyright owner of a song is entitled to royalties from each public performance.

In the nutshell, publishers become affiliated with BMI, ASCAP or SESAC, who in turn grant licenses to the music users, they then collect the royalties and fees and pay the publisher their share. Each of these organizations use their own unique approach in the calculation of royalties for their respective affiliates. Some of the factors include when and how the song was used and other research methods. Technology is also utilized in their process, including the Internet for tracking the use of songs online.

Songwriters can also join one of the three performing rights societies. Fortunately for the writers, the societies pay their performance income directly to them. The money does not go through the publisher first. Songwriters are only allowed to join one of the performing rights societies.

"Samples" are popular in the rap music world. If you plan to sample from a recording that already exists, you have to license both the publishing rights and the performance rights from the originating record company and publisher. There is no established, set fee. So you or your representation must negotiate the amount of money you must pay to secure the rights that you are seeking.

A "synchronization license" is commonly found when a song is used in a movie and the song is synchronized with the motion that the viewer can see on screen. Television commercials are another area where this type of license can be found. They key here is the use of music with images that are visual. Again, like with samples, fixed fees are not established with sync licenses. Songs also bring in revenue from the sale of sheet music and music folios and from record sales in foreign countries.

The music publisher must negotiate the amount of compensation before the license can be agreed to. Things to consider when discussing the sync fee include the capacity in which the song is being used and the budget of the project, be it a television show or movie. In conclusion, you should now know the basics about mechanical, performance and synchronization licenses. I encourage you to read more about music publishing when time permits. It's a fascinating and important subject for every songwriter, artist, manager and label.

MUSIC CONFERENCES

There are many music conferences and seminars across the United States each year. These are great events to market your project to industry executives and fans, all under the same roof. We must remember that the music business is all about people and personal relationships. Attending a music conference allows you to meet top industry representatives and executives. It allows you to shake their hand and personally hand them your CD. Some of the friendships and relationships that you will build at these events will last for years and years.

It's also a great place to learn about your chosen field. It's impossible to succeed in any business or industry if you don't know and understand the rules of the game and who the top players are.

It's not practical to attend all of the conferences, so how do you make a wise choice? I feel the key things to consider include:

- Location. The distance of the event from where you live.

- Which music industry executives will be attending as

speakers, panelists, mentors and scouts.

- The topics that will be covered in the educational segments of the event.

- Your opportunity to perform live during the "showcase" segment of the event.

- The cost of tickets for the event and other expenses such as food, fuel, hotel, parking, etc.

The common mistake I see musicians making at music conferences is not taking the daytime events seriously. Many people I speak with don't even bother attending the seminars, lectures and mentoring sessions. Or they only attend a small portion of those events. Their whole focus is on their "showcase" gig. While it's wonderful to have that opportunity and you should embrace it, make sure you remember to get the most you can out of the conference.

Go downstairs to the meeting rooms and sit in on the lectures. Give out CDs to industry pros. Network with other recording artists and try to work out some-mailing list and gig swapping deals. Partying all night and sleeping at the hotel all day until load in time at the concert venue is not doing your career much good. Make the most of this opportunity!

The other area that I would like to mention involves imposing on industry professionals while at music conferences. When pros attend these events, they should be there to meet artists, give advice, catch some shows and go home with a huge sack of CDs and press kits to review. They should, and the majority do, make themselves available during the day and at the showcase venues in the evening. This allows artists to approach, introduce themselves and respectfully submit a CD and press kit. If some executive or manager is grumpy and unapproachable, then perhaps they should have stayed home!

But if there's an industry professional that you want to meet and you see them at the hotel restaurant eating dinner with a spouse, friend or colleague, don't interrupt them to hand over a CD. Wait until you see them in a more "business-like" setting. It's a bit uncomfortable when a stranger approaches you for a chat while you're eating and your mouth is full of food, or their elbow is in your mashed potatoes as they reach across the table with the CD. There's a time and place for everything kids...

The other word of caution is not to bother executives in their hotel room. The A&R rep who spent the last ten hours speaking to musicians and is finally relaxing in his or her room with a glass of wine and their pajamas on, doesn't really want to hear a knock on their door at 11:30 p.m. Just have some patience and look to meet that person in the morning. I've heard labels executives, managers and other pros complain about this stuff countless times over the years.

A few years back at one of the bigger conferences, I had a band knocking on my hotel door at nearly midnight after finding out my room number from the front desk. I answered the door half asleep and there they are with an acoustic guitar in hand, ready to play me their new "hit" single.

I was tired and my voice was shot after talking all day. But since I'm an understanding person, I let their "audition" go on. After a few kind words, I went back to sleep. Many industry people would not have been so nice. The door would have been slammed in their face long before the first chord was played. (Just a little friendly advice to spare you from an awkward moment.)

One thing that I've seen many artists do, and I think it's a great idea by the way, is to send their CD and press kit to the industry pros before the event starts. It takes some work, but it seems to be a wise move. Most conferences list who will be speaking at their event well in advance on the official Web site. Some even include the person's Web site and/or e-mail address.

With some homework, you can find the address or e-mail of the label reps, managers, producers and other V.I.P.'s. Reach out to them with a note of introduction, or send over a CD and let them know when and where your showcase is. I listen to every CD that people send me in this manner. If I really dig the music, I will add them to the list of artists that I want to see while I'm in town. I respect their effort to get the music into the right hands.

There are many wonderful conferences and seminars across the country. However, my favorite events, in no particular order, are:

- New York, NY (C.M.J.)

- Austin, Texas (SXSW)

- Harrisburg, Pennsylvania (Millennium)

- Dewey Beach, Delaware (Dewey Beach Fest)

- Atlanta, Georgia (Atlantis)

- Boston, Massachusetts (NEMO)

RANDOM TIPS

I strongly urge you to open up a P.O. Box for your music-related mailing address. It is not a good idea these days to list a home address on your CD or Web site. If your act does take off on a grand scale, you don't want fans coming to your home and taking "souvenirs" such as your mailbox, welcome mat or lawn furniture.

Some of my major label clients and friends have made the mistake of using their home address on early demos. Years later, when they became famous, there would be dozens of people camped out on their front lawn at times, looking for everything from an autograph to a loan! It's wonderful to appreciate your fans, but you also have to guard your privacy, security and safety.

With solid planning, diligent research and lots of hard work, creating a buzz is not impossible, even for an artist that cannot afford a professional publicist to help them. The importance of a great press kit cannot be emphasized enough times. If you really want to make it in the music business, you have to be willing to work hard and invest money into your career. Compact discs, biographies and photos are not cheap – but they are necessary. If you want to be taken seriously by industry professionals, you must look and sound like a pro in every aspect of your presentation.

Before a record company is willing to take a chance on an act, they often want them to prove that consumers will be interested in the project. If an artist can sell a large number of CDs, secure a ton of airplay on college radio, and a good number of favorable press in music publications, while drawing a large audience to each of their performances, then labels may begin to show interest. There are never any guarantees, though. But at least you would be going about things in the correct manner.

Record companies are always looking for great new artists. They watch the ones that are creating a buzz in a given market. They usually know who is making the most noise in certain areas by keeping an eye on the music publications, the radio stations, and the bigger clubs.

Most labels do extensive A&R research to find a great artist before their competitor does and hits the jackpot. Record company executives also have a stable of contacts in the larger markets who tip them off on the hottest artists in town. This may include club owners, college radio program directors, lawyers and studio managers. Do your best so your name is the one they are talking about.

If you do not have the capital or the means to attempt a national campaign, all hope is not lost. You can start by choosing a large city as your target market. Later in this book I will list my favorite music cities across the country. You may live in one of these cities, or perhaps you're based in a nearby suburb. Make a list of everyone that you should be contacting in that market. Focus on college radio, newspapers, regional music magazines, clubs, record stores, booking agencies, managers and even commercial radio if they have a local music show. Start getting your name and material out to these people.

If the music is great and your plan is on target, you should start winning these people over and building a nice network of leads who are embracing your project. From there, just keep selling more and more CDs, drawing larger crowds at each show, forging strategic marketing alliances with the local universities and colleges and so on.

Basically, you must "own" your market. What I mean by that is make your original music project the most well known and successful one on the entire local scene. If you can pull this off in a big way, in a larger market, labels have ways of finding out about you.

A few months ago, I read a great article written by two of my clients, Blake Althen with Paula Bellenoit. Blake and Paula comprise Human Factor, a music production duo based in the Washington, DC area. I thought the article would be very helpful, so I asked if I could add it to my book. They graciously agreed, so here it is! Check out the following piece entitled, "The Power Of The Remix."

Artists pay thousands of dollars to promoters, consultants, managers, and producers to help get airplay, distribution, and of course making the music sound great. Hundreds of hours are spent on strategy planning, photo shoots, follow-up phone calls, rehearsals, websites, and traveling from site to site. Naturally enough, having spent money, time, and energy creating and marketing a song, the artists are fixed on their version of the song. Too often, therefore, they don't realize that, for relatively little money and virtually no effort on their part, they can have multiple re-mixes done and get their song heard by diverse new audiences that otherwise would never have been exposed to it. I am frequently perplexed. As I have said many times in my production workshops, why don't artists maximize their song's potential?

Most music projects (even entry level ones) start with some kind of plan. Of course, major and independent labels have more detailed plans than an individual artist, but the basic barebones plan is usually something like this:

- Write songs
- Hire a producer and get the songs recorded
- Get the CDs manufactured
- Make a music video (if budget allows)
- Hire a radio promoter/publicist to get airplay, interviews and press
- Go on tour to promote and sell the record

Simple and to the point, right? If only executing was so easy.

But it misses a simple and potentially lucrative step – the re-mix of the song into multiple genres. There should be a step added between steps 2 and 3:

Step 2 ½: Get the a cappella vocal tracks off to the re-mixer(s).

I think this is a crucial step and is overlooked by even the major labels at times.

WHY RE-MIX?

Most people have heard stories of major artists getting their original productions re-mixed by some very expensive and big named DJ. Sometimes labels will "leak" a re-mixed song that has not yet been released into the DJ record pools in order to get the buzz going about the track. Then the songs turn into dance sensations and explode into the club circuit helping to launch the artist into the pop world. Of course, that is a great goal, but I would prefer to give some examples of every day success stories and explain how to get a dance mix done for under $10,000.

CREATE "BUZZ" AT YOUR OWN SHOWS

Human Factor (Human Factor is the name of my production company) recently produced a really cool rock band. They did a rather catchy up-beat track at around 100 bpm (beats per minute) that had an adult contemporary/rock feel. Human Factor did a re-mix for them at 120 BPM that started rather subtly and gradually built up.

The group played their re-mix on the PA between sets and after their gigs. They figured every band plays music at intermission, why shouldn't the music be theirs? But they didn't want to play the same tunes people were about to hear or had just heard, so they got re-mixes. An interesting phenomenon occurred. People had just heard the songs and they were hearing them again. They found people just standing around dancing or listening with big smiles on their faces to the re-mixes. In many cases people in the audience would ask "What is this?" or, "Is this on the CD I just bought?" The artists would reply "Nope, but we'll give you a copy if you sign up for our mailing list." Dance tracks that were intended to be a filler between sets became a vehicle for getting more people signed up on the mailing list.

INCREASE YOUR EXPOSURE EVEN WHEN YOU'RE NOT PLAYING

At one of the group's gigs, there was a DJ between the sets. After the show, the DJ would play club tracks. The band's manager convinced the DJ to spin the bands re-mixes. It turned out the DJ loved the mixes. After the band's next set he immediately played the re-mixes and the audience continued to sing along with the songs. He told the band that their tracks were going to be in his set from now on.

Think about it like this: artists are performing every night. But an artist can only be in one place at one time... or can they? Put yourself in the artist's shoes. What if you are rocking a live gig in Spokane, Washington; at the same time, your dance tracks are being played in Miami, and your down beat mixes are thumping in Cincinnati? Your exposure just tripled. Likewise, there is no way a rock band is going to be able to play a gig in a dance club. But through re-mixing, the possibilities for a band are nearly endless.

These examples are just a couple creative ways independent artists generated "buzz" about their group and songs. But there are many more ways that solo artists, indie labels, and major labels use re-mixes to create buzz.

I find that many artists tend to record a song and put it in the proverbial can. I think now more than ever that mentality needs to be changed. While I agree that an artist should always be developing new material, I think that putting a song in the "can" should be replaced with Tupperware. You may want to come back and re-open the song for future mixes.

The more versions of a song you have the more chances you have of it being a success. I don't just mean that you should make club or dance mixes, acoustic versions are very powerful as well. Have you ever been in a dentist's office and heard the elevator music version of a rock song? Major recording artists didn't do those recordings just for fun. The more versions, the

126

more chances for royalties and exposure. They are trying to maximize their song's potential.

How to Re-mix?

You've heard some reasons why a re-mix can work for you; now, the next question is how do you get one done? Much like when you first start your music project, the first thing you may want to do is set a budget and some goals. Some artists may choose to attempt to hire the biggest name re-mixer they can get. Others may attempt to get an entire record of different mixes of the same one or two songs (tribal, dub, etc.) to send out to a DJ pool (I will talk about DJ pools in a moment). The important thing here is keeping in mind why you're going for it, and do what makes the most sense toward that goal.

What kind of Re-mix?

I mentioned a moment ago that some artists get an entire record of different mixes of the same song. Just as the rock scene has metal, alternative, emo, hair bands, nu-metal, classic rock, and many more sub genres; the club scene also has its own sub-genres: trance, tribal, house, dub, drum & bass, etc. A re-mix in each sub-genre will increase your chances of exposure. A DJ who plays a trance set will not play a house re-mix and vice-versa. It may ruin the mood of his set. If you have a mix for many sub-genre's, you have a chance with each DJ.

Here's a typical track list for a record of this type:

Track Listing
1. Keepers of our Souls (Original Edit) 3:20
2. Keepers of our Souls (DJ Blake's Filter Edit) 5:23
3. Keepers of our Souls (BA's Dub Mix) 7:75
4. Keepers of our Souls (BA's Tribal Mix) 9:23
5. Keepers of our Souls (DJ MRX Trance Mix) 9:54
6. Keepers of our Souls (DJ MRX Early Lounge Mix) 7:56
7. Keepers of our Souls (PMB's Anthem Mix) 8:59
8. Keepers of our Souls (BA's Soul Mix Extended) 10:32

9. Keepers of our Souls (BA's Soul Mix) 4:20

You may be thinking "Wow, how can I distinguish between the different club sub-genres when all I listen to is rock (or country, or pop, etc)?" At first they may all sound the same to you. They certainly did to me before I started paying close attention to the different musical genres. I remember talking to a re-mixer. I told him club music all sounded the same to me, THUMP THUMP THUMP THUMP!!!! He laughed, smiled and, knowing that I had a resume full of rock music, said some people think all rock music sounds the same, some dude yelling and too much guitar.

That got me curious and I began to familiarize myself with many different sub genres. Of course, the only way to do that is to take the time to listen to the music. Since I can't include a CD in this article, I posted up a few examples on the company's Web site. http://humanfactor.net/remix

PICKING A DJ OR RE-MIXER

Once you have your project goals and budget set down, it's time to find your re-mixer. There are many DJ's in just about every metropolitan city that will re-mix your track. Prices range from free to $10,000.00+ for a re-mix.

Why would anyone do it for free? The first reason is probably the simplest. They love your song. The next is somebody who is new at re-mixing and they are trying to get their feet wet and build a resume. You can go this route for an initial experience, but, as in most things, you get what you pay for.

The process for selecting re-mixers is very similar to that of finding a producer for the "main" mix. Unfortunately there is no Bureau of Producers Licensing Department. To become a re-mixer you need a computer, speakers and a business card that says John Doe: Re-mixer. This means there are many re-mixers out there today. You will have to do your own research. Ask them for a sample of their work, credits, and maybe even references. Many re-mixers are also DJ's. In that instance, check out their set in a club, they will probably play a fair share of their own re-mixes.

Certain DJs report their club playlists to charts (such as Billboard). This may be of interest if you are interested in getting on the charts, but call the chart the DJ reports to and ask them if they have ever heard of him or her. Above all, remember: when the truth is told, let the music do the talking.

So, the first thing you do to pick your re-mixer is decide whose music you like the most. Or try to get the biggest "brand name" DJ you can afford. If you care about getting on the charts, ask the DJ if they report to any of them. Do your homework. Do some research by at least going out to a few different clubs; you don't have to stay long. You will find that different clubs attract a different audience and a different audience may attract a different sound. Try to experience the music the way the audience will. Don't stand in the corner with a notepad. Go the club with friends. Remember that the people on the dance floor may be celebrating something or they may just be out for a night on the town. They may have even had a couple of drinks. Perhaps you may want to join them – just to understand the music more.

Re-mix Tips

When it comes to how to make a re-mix there is no set of rules. However I can tell you what some of the elements of a successful re-mix are. First, as in pop, catchy and big hooks are always a plus. The more the audience can recognize the chorus the better. The second tip is a bit trickier. You want the energy of the song to climax and then come down. Good dance music ebbs and flows like the cycles in nature. Remember people are dancing to this. You need to give them a break to catch their breath so they can go full speed again.

A third element not to forget is your target audience. What may go over very well in NYC may not do so well in Madrid. Again, do your research. Finally, another element you need to consider is that a DJ has to be able to cross-fade into and out of your re-mix. So, a good re-mix will have a few measures of naked beat (very little-to-no pitch) at the beginning and the ending. The DJ uses those measures to synch it up with the outtro of the previous track and have a smooth and seamless transition from one song to the next.

After the Re-mix Is Done

OK. Now you have a screaming re-mix of your current favorite song. What do you do with it? I had mentioned DJ record pools. In a nutshell, record pools are companies that provide music to club DJs, and in return, the DJs report results back to them. Record labels use them as a source of information on what is working in the clubs. Obviously, record pools can be a crucial part of making a dance mix a success.

In writing this article, I had a rather extensive conversation with an executive at a top record pool. He told me that labels are tightening their belts and not servicing as many of the record pools. What is "servicing" a record pool? That means providing them multiple copies of your re-mix so they can make it available to the DJs in their pool. He also illustrated the importance of vinyl. There is still widespread opinion that vinyl "just sounds better." And of course, he made sure to remind me that songs had to have a nice intro and outro. See? I wasn't lying to you before. The last tip he gave me was for hip hop. He seemed to think that having a clean edit (no profanity) was a good idea. I happen to agree.

I feel that some artists need to get over their fear of the unknown. I have had singer/songwriter clients do every thing from giggle to look at me like I am speaking a foreign language when I ask, "Are you planning on having this re-mixed"?

It may be surprising at first, but believe me, once you hear your song in a club and see 2000 happy people jumping around to your beat, your mind will be changed. So take a chance, try something new – just go for it. You are an artist. Act like one and be a little different. Maximize your song's potential.

BLAKE ALTHEN and PAULA BELLENOIT are the record production duo known as Human Factor. They've worked with Michael Manring and DJ Logic, and have produced artists such as SONiA, Rachel Panay, Jennifer Cutting and AbbySomeOne. Human Factor is also known as one of the industry's leading clinicians, providing dynamic and interactive seminars and clinics both at music conferences and independently. Visit www.hfproductions.com.

ALTERNATIVE CAREER OPTIONS

There are many talented musicians and singers who have no aspirations of being an artist signed to a record company. There are numerous ways to earn a living with your musical abilities without being under contract to a label. However, some people do use various career alternatives as a way to finance, supplement or advance their original music projects.

Cover bands often make a great deal of money. Wedding bands can earn over $3,000 a night. Some clubs pay pop and rock music cover bands over $1,500 a night. Being in such a band may be a way for you to earn money, while using your musical abilities in a productive manner. People in cover bands often mention how much fun they have while performing. The atmosphere at clubs and wedding receptions are usually energetic and upbeat. It's also a great way for new people to see your act in action. You never know when someone in the crowd might be interested in hiring you for their own upcoming function.

Teaching people how to sing or to play a musical instrument is another suggestion. Teaching can be fun and rewarding. Many local music shops offer lessons and good teachers are always in demand. In addition to the financial gains, being an active part of your local music community is a great way to meet other musicians and songwriters. This can lead to friendships, co-writing projects and even session work.

Producing is another idea that may be beneficial, if you have the knowledge, skills and experience. If you possess the ability to work the equipment in a recording studio, the ear to produce an act and an interest in production, you should consider this option. Many up-and-coming artists need a producer to assist them in polishing up their material and getting the right sound in the studio. If you are an excellent songwriter, your production projects may even be an opportunity to place some of your material with the acts that you produce.

Once you have some experience, you can play a sample of your production work for potential clients. If they like the sound that you were able to get for another act, they may be interested in hiring you for their project. Recording studios are often frequented by musicians, managers and record company personnel. It's a great way to network and meet other people in the music industry who may be interested in your services.

Many songwriters contact music publishers and personal managers in an attempt to place songs with established recording artists. If you have material that would be suitable for another artist to record, your representatives can shop your CD to various publishers, managers, producers and record companies, in an effort to place a song with a signed act.

This is a great way to make a name for yourself should you be fortunate enough to get one of your songs cut. In addition to any potential financial benefits, you may find some doors opening up as your reputation as a great songwriter begins to grow. TV networks and motion picture studios often need music for their projects. This can be yet another way to get your music in a position to earn you money. Top entertainment attorneys, agents and managers have contacts to get your songs into the right hands.

Excellent songwriters are always in demand, and some music publishers will hire talented ones to write exclusively for them. Under the right circumstances, this can be a great opportunity. You should look for a company that will pay you a fair salary and proper royalties (should any become due) and one that will actively pitch your songs to the best opportunities. Some publishers will even assist you in getting your demos recorded. There are many variations of these songwriter contracts, so be sure to seek the guidance of an entertainment lawyer before negotiating or signing anything. You want to make sure that your interests are protected and that you are being properly compensated.

Engineering and mixing are other options for those who have the proper skills and experience. Recording studios and artists often look for skilled engineers and mixers to assist them during sessions. It's also another way for you to become an active member of your local music community, while networking your talents to others.

If you are a proficient and versatile singer or musician, being a session player may be of interest to you. An example would be when an artist needs a background vocalist or a guitar player to contribute to a recording session. The pay is usually very good, and the networking possibilities are excellent. It is important to let musicians, songwriters, managers and recording studios know that you are available for session work. Place advertisements in music publications describing your abilities. Interested parties can later call you to discuss the details, such as your fees and availability. Songwriters, solo artists and music groups often rely on session musicians and singers to complete their demos.

You should have a demo CD, a discography and a biography available for any potential clients. This will give interested parties the opportunity to hear your talents and determine if you are suitable for their project. If you are able to build a reputation as a great session player, word will get around.

Working on a project as a session musician can be financially rewarding. The music community in most areas is tight-knit.

It seems like everyone knows everyone. If you can make a name for yourself, it can often lead to steady work and a handsome income. If you are a versatile singer or player, who can perform in several genres, you can do even better.

Working at a music store is another possibility. If you know about musical equipment such as instruments, amplifiers, keyboards, recording gear and effects, you could be a big asset to their staff. Most shops even offer discounts to employees. Music stores, in some cases, allow staff members to have long hair, visible tattoos and dress in a manner that would probably not be acceptable in the corporate world. This is important to artists that have a certain image for their music career but still need a day job to pay the bills.

As you can see, there are many ways to be part of your local music community. Regardless of your goals as a songwriter or musician, your musical abilities should allow you to advance your career, while earning a respectable living. Meeting other people in the business can help your career and even provide you with new and diverse opportunities. You never know what label executive, producer or manager is going to walk into a studio while you're there doing your thing.

Being an active member of your music scene can help you in many ways. The music industry is based on whom you know and who knows you. Make sure that your name is recognized as someone on their way to the top.

Record companies and music publishers are also excellent places to seek employment. It's a great opportunity to learn more about the business, while meeting industry leaders and gaining valuable experience. If you are more interested in other areas of the business, you could then seek job opportunities at booking agencies, artist management companies or publicity firms. Working at any of those businesses could also be helpful to the aspiring musician. Try to learn and network as much as you possibly can. There are many excellent Web sites that list job openings and can be a valuable resource for you. Monster.com and Hotjobs.com are two great places to begin your search.

MY TOP 40 MARKETS

I'm often asked by clients which venues, radio stations and newspapers are my favorites in a given market. I appreciate that people respect my opinion regarding what's really special out there. Below, you will find a list of the 39 markets that I feel have the best original music scenes across the United States. For the fortieth market, I included Toronto, Canada, which has a solid original scene in its own right.

I will list venues, radio stations and publications that I think are doing a great job and deserve to be recognized as among the best in what they do. Since this book will be read by people who create music in a variety of musical genres, each of the listings below will not be for everyone.

As you are researching a market, visit the Web site of the venue/radio station/publication and determine if they embrace your genre of music. While on their respective sites, you should be able to find the correct contact name, mailing address, phone number and in some cases, even their submission rules and procedures.

It's also a good idea to keep up-to-date with information on these people. Radio stations change formats and venues regularly close down or change the musical style that they book Research is key - and the Internet is a wonderful, free tool for those efforts.

ATLANTA
- Venues: Dark Horse Tavern – Café 290 – Smith's Olde Bar
- Radio Stations: WREK
- Press: Creative Loafing

BALTIMORE
- Venues: Fletcher's – Ram's Head Tavern – Recher Theatre
- Radio Stations: WNUC – WMBC
- Press: Baltimore Sun – Music Monthly

BIRMINGHAM
- Venues: The Nick – Zydeco
- Radio Stations: WRAX
- Press: Birmingham News

BOSTON
- Venues: The Middle East – T.T. The Bear's Place-Paradise – Harper's Ferry
- Radio Stations: WZBC – WBRS – WERS
- Press: Boston Globe – Boston Phoenix – Boston Herald

CHARLOTTE
- Venues: Tremont Music Hall – Double Door Inn
- Radio Stations: WXYC – WKNC – WGWG
- Press: Creative Loafing – Charlotte Observer

CHICAGO
- Venues: The Elbo Room – House of Blues – Metro – The Note – Abbey Pub
- Radio Stations: WNUR – WHPK
- Press: Chicago Tribune – Illinois Entertainer – Chicago Sun-Times

CLEVELAND
- Venues: The Hi-Fi Club – The Odeon – The Grog Shop
- Radio Stations: WRUW – WCSB
- Press: Cleveland Scene – Free Times

CINCINNATI
- Venues: Top Cats – Bogart's
- Radio Stations: WAQZ
- Press: Cincinnati City Beat – Revue Magazine

DALLAS
- Venues: Trees – Club Dada – Curtain Club – Gypsy Tea Room
- Radio Stations: KTCU
- Press: Dallas Observer – Dallas Morning News

DENVER
- Venues: Bluebird Theater – 15th Street Tavern – Rock Island Club – Lion's Lair
- Radio Stations: KVCU – KUVO
- Press: Denver Post - Westword

DETROIT
- Venues: St. Andrews Hall – Lager House – The Blind Pig
- Radio Stations: WCBN – WDBM
- Press: Detroit Free Press – Real Detroit Weekly

HOUSTON
- Venues: Walter's – Ole Moulton Bank – Continental Club – Engine Room
- Radio Stations: KTRU
- Press: Houston Press – Houston Chronicle

INDIANAPOLIS
- Venues: Melody Inn – Birdy's – CT Peppers
- Radio Stations: WECI
- Press: Indianapolis Star – NUVO

KANSAS CITY, MO
- Venues: Davey's Uptown Ramblers Club – The Hurricane
- Radio Stations: KKFI
- Press: Pitch Weekly

LOS ANGELES
- Venues: Dragon Fly – Genghis Cohen – The Gig in Hollywood – The Roxy
- Radio Stations: KSCR – KROQ
- Press: Los Angeles Times – L.A. Weekly

LOUISVILLE
- Venues: Stevie Ray's Blues Bar – Headliners
- Radio Stations: WLCV
- Press: The Courier Journal – Louisville Eccentric Observer

MEMPHIS
- Venues: Rum Boogie Café – The Stage Stop – Blue City Café
- Radio Stations: WEVL
- Press: The Memphis Flyer – Commercial Appeal

MIAMI
- Venues: Churchill's – Tobacco Road – Crobar
- Radio Stations: WVUM
- Press: Miami New Times – Miami Herald

MILWAUKEE
- Venues: Cactus Club – The Rave – Mad Planet
- Radio Stations: WLUM – WWSP
- Press: Shepherd Express – Milwaukee Journal Sentinel

MINNEAPOLIS
- Venues: 7th Street Entry – Lee's Liquor Lounge – Fine Line Music Café
- Radio Stations: KUOM
- Press: Star Tribune – City Pages

NASHVILLE
- Venues: Bluebird Café – The Sutler
- Radio Stations: WANT – WMTS
- Press: The Tennessean – Music Row

NEW ORLEANS
- Venues: House of Blues – Tipitina's – Checkpoint Charlie's
- Radio Stations: KFTE – KRVS
- Press: OffBeat Magazine – Gambit Weekly

NEW YORK
- Venues: CBGB's – Arlene Grocery – Cutting Room
  – Blue Note – Kenny's Castaways – The Lion's Den
  – Iridium – Knitting Factory – Mercury Lounge
- Radio Stations: WFUV – WRHU – WNYU – WRSU
  – WMCX
- Press: Village Voice – Daily News – New York Times
  – The Aquarian

OKLAHOMA CITY
- Venues: Green Door – The Deli – Conservatory
- Radio Stations: KRSC
- Press: The Daily Oklahoman

OMAHA
- Venues: O'Leavers Pub – Ranch Bowl
- Radio Stations: KDNE – KFKX
- Press: Omaha World Herald

ORLANDO
- Venues: The Social – House of Blues
- Radio Stations: WFIT
- Press: Orlando Weekly

PHILADELPHIA
- Venues: Grape Street Pub – The Khyber – Pontiac Grille
  – North Star Bar
- Radio Stations: WXPN – WKDU – WLVR
- Press: Philadelphia Weekly – The City Paper

PHOENIX
- Venues: Emerald Lounge – Rhythm Room
- Radio Stations: KASC
- Press: Phoenix New Times

PITTSBURGH
- Venues: Quiet Storm – Moondog's – 31st Street Pub
- Radio Stations: WRCT
- Press: City Paper – Pittsburgh Post-Gazette

PORTLAND, OR
- Venues: Crystal Ballroom – Aladdin Theater
  – Meow Meow – Berbati's Pan
- Radio Stations: KPSU
- Press: Portland Mercury – Willamette Week

PROVIDENCE
- Venues: The Living Room – The Blackstone – Olive's
- Radio Stations: WBSR – WDOM
- Press: Providence Phoenix – Providence Journal

SALT LAKE CITY
- Venues: Liquid Joe's – Kilby Court – Ego's
- Radio Stations: KSUU – KAGJ
- Press: SLUG Magazine – Salt Lake City Weekly

SAN ANTONIO
- Venues: White Rabbit – Triple Crown
- Radio Stations: KSYM
- Press: San Antonio Current

SAN DIEGO
- Venues: The Casbah – Winston's Beach Club
- Radio Stations: XTRA
- Press: San Diego Reader

SAN FRANCISCO
- Venues: The Fillmore – El Rio – DNA Lounge
  – Café Du Nord
- Radio Stations: KUSF – KALX
- Press: San Francisco Weekly – San Francisco Bay Guardian

SEATTLE
- Venues: Chop Suey – Conor Byrne's – Catwalk Club
  – The Funhouse
- Radio Stations: KUGS – KAOS – KMTT
- Press: Seattle Times – The Stranger

ST. LOUIS
- Venues: The Way Out Club – Hi-Pointe – Off Broadway
- Radio Stations: KWUR
- Press: The Riverfront Times

TAMPA
- Venues: Skipper's Smokehouse – Jannus Landing
- Radio Stations: WUTZ
- Press: Tampa Tribune – The Weekly Planet

TORONTO
- Venues: The Guvernment – Horseshoe Tavern
- Radio Stations: CIUT – CKLN
- Press: Eye Weekly – Toronto Life Magazine

WASHINGTON, DC
- Venues: The Black Cat – 9:30 Club – Grog & Tankard
- Radio Stations: WCUA
- Press: The Washington Post

NATIONAL PRESS

Here's a list of magazines that I really enjoy and respect their efforts. I have organized some by the genre that they focus on the most. Others are in a more "general" list. Check out their Web sites and try to get your music to the appropriate publications.

ROCK
Metal Edge
Metal Maniacs
Revolver

URBAN
Black Beat
Vibe
XXL

JAZZ
Down Beat
Jazz Times
Jazziz

BLUES
Blues Revue
Blue Suede News
Living Blues

SINGER/SONGWRITER
Amplifier Magazine
Dirty Linen
Paste
Utne

PUNK
Amp Magazine
Maximum Rock n Roll
Outburn
Thrasher

GUITAR/BASS/DRUMS
Guitar Player
Guitar World
Bass Player
Modern Drummer

GENERAL INDUSTRY
TOPICS
Billboard
Blender
CMJ New Music Report
CMJ New Music Monthly
Electronic Musician
Hits
Musico Pro
Radio & Records
Rolling Stone

Artists often ask me if it's all worth it. The answer is a resounding yes! Some people are born with a gift to write or play music. Others, though not as innately talented, are able to compensate through their drive and ambition.

Forming a music group is difficult, because you must find three or four people who have the same calling and passion that you do. You also have to find people who you can get along with personally under difficult situations. This is not always an easy task. Band member often seem to be coming and going. Any of you that have been in bands know how hard it is to keep a steady lineup. When you are successful in doing this, it may seem like magic. Songs begin to come together and your live performances get more and more polished.

Some people prefer to work as a solo act or duo for whatever reason. That direction certainly can cut down on the fights, creative differences and ego-fueled battles. Regardless of how you present yourself, the music business is driven by hopes and dreams. Some people are fortunate enough to see their dreams become a reality. Doing everything right still does not guarantee success, but it will certainly increase your chances!

Learn all that you can about the music industry. Read books, attend seminars, talk to other people in the business and keep improving your songs. Do not ever underestimate the importance of your songs, because high-quality material is what drives the music business.

After your songs have reached their full potential, make sure that your live show and press kit are professional and ready to go. After that, continue your search for a manager, producer, lawyer and booking agent. You must realize the importance of having professionals guiding your career. Their experience, knowledge and contacts can do wonders for your project. When you find honest, hard working, and competent music industry professionals to assist you, let them do their job so you can concentrate on yours. If you try to do everything on your own, you'll be spending too much time handling the business end of things. The creative and performance aspects of your career will suffer. Your main focus should be on writing, rehearsing and performing.

An entertainment attorney or an agent will be the first of your advisors. Make sure that you hire someone who has experience and contacts in the music business. Many entertainment attorneys offer career guidance to artists who don't have a personal manager. In some cases, they can help you approach a personal manager and negotiate any contracts that may be offered.

You should never sign or agree to anything without the guidance of an entertainment attorney. I've repeated that many times in this book because of the importance of that advice. There are too many horror stories of artists and labels making decisions in haste, without the proper guidance and then regretting it for years. Please don't make that mistake.

Try to find a personal manager who has the experience and knowledge to successfully guide your career. Make sure that you can communicate easily with your manager. You must work together as a team, and it's important they understand and embrace your vision for the future. Each and every manager has their own style and way of conducting business. You will be working closely with this person, so try to choose someone whose personality is compatible with yours. If you prefer to conduct business in a calm, professional manner, you may feel uncomfortable with a manager whose style is loud, aggressive and pushy. On the other hand, some people may want a manager like that!

A booking agent will also be an integral part of your team. It is very important to perform live as much as possible. A good booking agent will do all that they can to get you steady gigs. They should work hard at negotiating a fair and reasonable price for your services. As you build a following, your booking agent should get you into bigger and better paying venues, as well. The booking agent may even have contacts that could help you secure an opening slot on a hot regional or national tour.

Touring is an important part of an artist's career. An active booking agent and personal manager should do all they can to keep you on stage as much as possible. It's a great way to promote your act, increase record sales and increase your fan base.

Tours early in your career may not be money makers, but you will be laying down the foundation for your future. As time goes on, you should begin to play better venues and receive more money for your performances. Your means of traveling and accommodations should also improve over time.

When it comes to recording your demo, an experienced producer should be hired. Before hiring one, you should ask to hear a sample of previous production work. Regardless of the deal you negotiate regarding their fee, make sure that you work with someone who understands your style and direction. You should seek someone who will enhance your sound and not try to change it to what they want.

Remember, they are working for you, so don't be afraid to speak up if they are pushing you into dramatically changing your sound. Make sure that you have the final say, because it's your career that's on the line. With the popularity these days of home recording equipment, I'm noticing a trend where more and more people who send me a demo produced it themselves. In some cases, it sounds great. Those people have clearly mastered the skill of getting the best sounds from their gear.

I have also heard many self-produced demos that are quite weak. Be honest with yourself. Does your demo really reflect the sound and the vision that you have for your music? If it doesn't, then it's time to start interviewing producers. Great producers can bring so much to the table. Don't underestimate their potential contributions. Listen to their suggestions, but make up your own mind. Before you manufacture CDs, make sure that you Master the songs. Don't cut corners and press up songs that have not been mastered. There is a difference in quality and industry people, especially radio and record company executives, will hear it.

A publicist is another person who can be beneficial to your career. A good publicist will be able to get you press and media coverage. Favorable reviews and articles are essential for your press kit. So are television appearances. It's important to be seen and heard as often as possible. If you cannot afford a publicist at this time, you and your advisors will have to assume those responsibilities. Make sure that you do your best, from your presentation to the follow up. Don't forget that a weak or amateur looking press kit is almost as bad as no press kit at all. I'm not kidding. Don't forget the two-pocket portfolio to house everything!

Radio promoters are another avenue that many artists use to increase their buzz. It's vital that you secure radio airplay for your CD at the appropriate college radio stations. If someone on your advisory team does not have contacts at various radio stations, and your budget allows it, hire a professional radio promoter. At some point, I hope your career evolves to the point of being successful on both college and commercial radio stations. Shop around for someone with a good track record and a thorough knowledge of the business and your genre. Make sure they regularly keep you or your manager posted on their efforts and accomplishments concerning your project.

Photographers are a big part of communicating your image to the public. A good photographer will listen to your music and talk with you in an effort to better understand your vision and direction. They can use their creative skills to photograph you in a manner that will highlight your image. You should interview several photographers before hiring one. Take a look at some of their previous work and talk with them to see if you communicate well together. A successful photo shoot can yield great results for the visual aspects of your career, but a poor one can be a waste of time and money.

When it's time for your advisors to approach record companies, make sure that you target labels that are right for you. Indies and majors both have pros and cons. You have to determine your needs and what they can and cannot offer you. Remember that it's about the right deal – not just any deal!

At times, artists and managers approach me, hoping I can help jumpstart their career after they came up short during the initial shopping efforts they did on their own. When I review a list of the labels they shopped to, I often shake my head in amazement. Rap music going to rock labels, jazz going to blues labels.... I've seen people do that and worse. Please do your homework if you are trying to shop on your own or with your manager – or better yet, bring in a professional that will do it the right way. Especially with so few labels willing to accept unsolicited material these days. You may have to hire a professional if you expect your music to get reviewed.

All because some small indie in the Midwest accepts unsolicited music, it doesn't mean that you have to send them a package. Make sure you are compatible with their roster and direction, or save your money and press kit. This is a common mistake that should not be so common!

As you consider labels, take into consideration such things as distribution, their commitment and enthusiasm towards your project, artistic control, advance money, tour support, video budget and promotional capabilities. Make sure that your entertainment attorney reviews and negotiates your contract. Recording contracts are quite lengthy and very complex. Their experience and knowledge can be very helpful.

Take your time, plan things out carefully and work hard. If music is what you really want to do, then go for it. It's a wonderful way to make a living, if you are fortunate enough to find success with it.

With the increasing complexity of life and the sheer volume of information that we must process each day, it's no surprise that people find it so difficult to successfully balance their personal and professional agendas. If you work hard towards a goal and it does not work out favorably, you must re-evaluate both the information and effort that went into your plan, along with your original expectations. To maintain a high level of objectivity, seek a dose of reality from a person that you respect and who's not directly involved in your project.

Ask yourself if you really did all of the necessary preparation and planning that is needed to execute such a large and important plan. Determine if you were honest and realistic when you assessed the situation, back on day one of the planning phase. Have you recognized your personal agenda and balanced that with the project's ultimate agenda and goals?

Have you considered and contemplated every option available to you, during the planning and implementation stages of your campaign? Ask yourself if you truly sought the professional advice and guidance that is needed in planning such an important chapter of your career.

And finally, ask yourself if you are mature enough to accept the responsibility for any consequences for your actions or inactions, regardless if the outcome is favorable or a failure? Have you shown originality in your planning? Can you allow yourself to dream, while maintaining a clear view of reality? Do you believe in yourself and those around you, without reservation?

Either you or a member of your advisory team must take the necessary steps to face uncertainty, while developing a strong level of foresight and vision. The music business is going through unprecedented change these days. You must figure out your plan and your place in this business, or you will be swept away quickly. Avoid falling into a trap based on previous experiences. If you made a mistake, fix it, learn from it and move on!

Research for accurate information and look to successful and tested assumptions before you make a final decision while formulating your plan. Challenge your creativity so you can reach new and exciting levels of evolvement. Each original thought that you have is creative. The trick is coming up with original thoughts that other people find equally interesting and unique. As you devise your plan, force yourself to come up with numerous ideas and goals. Not just the obvious ones. Sure, get the obvious ideas down on paper, but keep challenging yourself to think outside of the box. How else can you promote your music? Where else can you perform? How can you get your records into the hands of consumers?

Recording artists and record companies that employ creative strategies, along with battle tested traditional methods of conducting business, have a significant advantage over their competition. Being creative makes a project more enjoyable and this sense of happiness leads to greater achievement, more production and a higher morale for everyone on your team. When I say creative, it's far deeper than just songwriting or graphic design, but creative in your approach towards reaching your career objectives.

Everyone has their own definition of success. Some people equate success with how much money they earn and the material possessions that income can buy them. Other people define success as doing what they want to do and being happy with one's career and life in general. I feel that if you love what you do for a living and you are earning enough money to pay your bills and be a responsible member of society, then you're a success in my book.

Hopefully this book has been a learning experience for you. I strongly encourage you to read as much as you can about the music business. Knowledge and persistence are the keys to achieving your goals in any area of life. It's a waste of time and money to keep spinning your wheels by making the same mistakes over and over. If music truly is your career choice, then do not hesitate to study hard and surround yourself with knowledgeable professionals.

Do not be discouraged if you find that you have made some errors along the way. Just be mature enough to admit your mistakes and strong enough to overcome any bad choices. Your greatest steps towards furthering your career will come when you learn to blend the development and presentation of your talent with your knowledge and understanding of how the business works.

Create great music, build a solid team, design an intelligent plan and work hard to make it a reality. That's what it comes down to, my friend.

I have one last bit of advice to give you. Please protect your ears. Hearing loss is a serious issue facing musicians and anyone exposed to loud sounds. Take the steps necessary to guard your precious ears.

Thank you for spending some time with this book. Good luck and may all of your dreams come true!

Advance: When a record company or publisher pays a writer or an artist a sum of money and then holds back the royalties until that money is repaid through record sales.

A&R Department (Artists and Repertoire): Record company executives whose primary duty is to discover and develop new artists. They help in song selection and finding the right producer for their acts. The A&R representative also acts as the liaison between the artist and the record company.

Bootleggers: A person who illegally manufactures artist merchandise, such as T-shirts, without permission.

Brand: A name or a design that distinguishes a product from its competitors.

Business Manager: A person whose primary duty is to handle the financial aspects of an artist's career, such as keeping track of income, expenses and taxes.

Cold Calling: Contacting someone that you do not know to pitch your product or service. For example, "cold calling" a radio station or concert venue to pitch your music group.

Controlled Composition Clause: When a record company tries to control the rate paid for publishing rights. Generally this winds up at three-quarters of the standard fee.

Co-Publish: When two or more parties own the publishing rights to the same song.

Copyright: Legal rights granting the creator of a work the power to control aspects such as publishing, reproducing, and selling.

Cover Song: When an artist records a song that was written and released by another artist in the past.

Cross-Collateralization: When the financial losses from one record are deducted from the profits earned by another record.

Crossover: When a song is successful in more than one category of music. An example would be a song that is successful on the pop charts and the country charts at the same time.

Decline: When sales of a product are diminishing with little or no prospect of that downward trend shifting for the better.

Demo: A recording of a song or songs, for the purpose of showcasing the skills of an artist, musician, singer or writer.

Derivative Work: A new work based on, or derived from, another work.

Follow Up: A key part of the sales process in which leads are contacted to assess their interest in a given project.

Key Man Clause: A clause in an agreement that allows an artist to leave a record company or manager if the key man leaves.

Logo: A symbol or design that represents a company or a product.

Mechanical License: A record company secures this license from a publisher, giving them the right to include a song on a record.

MIDI: Musical Instrument Digital Interface

One-Stop: A business that purchases records from a variety of record companies, then later sells them to smaller stores that cannot get records directly from the labels themselves.

P.O.P.: A Point Of Purchase is a display that is meant to bring attention to a product and persuade consumers to purchase it. P.O.P. displays are often near the cash register to attract the attention of people as they wait in line.

Pressing & Distribution Deals: P&D Deals are agreements where a large record company manufactures and distributes CDs from a smaller label. In most cases, the small indie label is responsible for promoting and marketing the release.

Press Release: Generally a brief document sent to the press to announce an important event, such as a new CD or a tour.

Public Domain: A song with an expired or invalid copyright. It can also be a song with a lapsed copyright.

Query: A letter asking someone for their permission to submit a song or press kit. Artists frequently send query letters to record companies and music publishers asking permission to submit a CD or review.

Rack Jobber: Someone who rents space in a department store and sells records on racks. The rack jobber delivers records to the individual stores, determines which releases to stock, and earns money from the records sold.

Recoupment: When royalties are withheld to recover certain monies which were advanced to — or spent on — a writer or an artist.

Recession: A period where economic activity is sluggish and weak.

Road Manager: Person responsible for ensuring that things run smoothly during a tour. Some of their duties include booking hotels, arranging ground and air transportation and collecting the money after each performance. They also oversee the road crew, including the sound and light technicians. The road manager handles any day-to day problems that occur during the tour so the artist can concentrate on performing and promotion.

Rotation: The number of times a song is played on a radio station in a day. The three most common categories of rotation are light, medium, and heavy.

Sales Forecast: A prediction of the income your business will earn in a certain period of time.

S.A.S.E: A self-addressed stamped envelope.

Solicited: When a music industry professional requests a demo from another party. An example would be when a record company calls a personal manager and asks for a CD after reading a great review about an artist in a magazine.

Target Market: A segment of consumers who have similar needs and interests to whom a product or service is marketed, based on that group's strong possibility of becoming a customer.

Unsolicited: When a demo is sent to a music industry professional who did not request it. Unsolicited CDs are usually returned to the sender unopened, or destroyed.

ARTIST NAME

Mike Smith – Vocals
John Jones – Bass
Sarah King – Guitar
Tom Martin – Drums

"Melodic Pop/Rock Group Based in New York City"   www.EnterYourWebsiteHere.com

Fact Sheet

RADIO

WFUV	New York, NY	WCVE	Richmond, VA
WXPN	Philadelphia, PA	WICN	Worcester, MA
KINK	Portland, OR	WSMU	N. Dartmouth, MA
WMWV	Conway, NH	KGOU	Norman, OK
WBFO	Buffalo, NY	WTJU	Charlottesville, VA
WUSM	Hattiesburg, MS	WUTC	Chattanooga, TN
WRFG	Atlanta, GA	WMNF	Tampa, FL
WUSR	Scranton, PA	WMPG	Portland, ME
WORT	Madison, WI	KZUM	Lincoln, NE
WDVX	Knoxville, TN	WPFW	Washington, DC
KIOS	Omaha, NE	WDHA	Cedar Knolls, NJ
WGLT	Normal, IL	WNTI	Hackettstown, NJ
WMPR	Jackson, MS	WFDU	Teaneck, NJ

PRESS

"The melodies are catchy, the songs very well written and their performances a delight."
— *Midwest Star Journal Tribune*

"A large and enjoyable dose of timeless old-school pop."
— *New York Daily Times*

"Great songs, a solid live show, the next big thing!"
— *Los Angeles Post Gazette*

VENUES

- Mercury Lounge – New York City
- Toad's Place – New Haven, CT
- The Whiskey Bar – Hoboken, NJ
- Double Door – Chicago, IL

- The Bitter End – New York City
- The Middle East – Cambridge, MA
- North Star Bar – Philadelphia, PA
- 9:30 Club – Washington, DC

INTERNET

- Official Web Site: 5,000 hits per month
- MySpace: 2,500 Friends

CONTACT

- 212.555.1212
- MikeSmith@YourEmailAddress.com

"Eugene Foley is a key asset to the world of emerging music, a consummate professional not only with regard to the insight into and execution of his craft but the manner in which he approaches all that he does. More importantly, he is indeed rare in this business of music because his expertise is matched by his honesty, common sense and passion. Young artists — especially at this crossroads of the business — would do well to tap into his experience and understanding of how to make it in the 21st Century music biz." **Robert Haber – Founder & CEO of College Music Journal (C.M.J.) Network, Publisher of New Music Report & New Music Monthly and Producer of the CMJ Music Marathon**

"Every musician I've referred to Eugene has been thrilled with his help, and thanked me afterwards. That, to me, says it all." **Derek Sivers – President and Programmer – CD Baby and HostBaby**

"Eugene Foley is one of the most well rounded, experienced, and knowledgeable people that you will find in the music industry. From his experience working with labels, distribution, public relations, management, marketing and just about every facet of the music industry, you just can't go wrong by having him on your team." **John Seymour – Grammy Award winning Producer/Engineer/ Mixer whose credits include: U2, Dave Matthews, Santana, Vertical Horizon & Mighty Mighty Bosstones**

"Aspiring artists looking for a competitive advantage in the music industry today need look no further than Eugene Foley. His insight and breadth of knowledge is rare." **Greg Johnson – A&R Executive – Lava/Atlantic Records**

"Eugene is an exceptional music man. His ear for a great song and his ability to work so successfully with artists and labels make him a rare asset in today's music business." **Mark Mazzetti – Former Vice President of A&R at A&M Records**

"There's a revolution going on in the Music Industry. Today more than ever Artists need to be educated and surround themselves with knowledgeable and capable professionals who know what's most important in developing their career. Eugene Foley is a very valuable asset to any artist he works with. Not only does he bring an exceptional depth of knowledge and experience to his work, but he does it with a level of integrity and honesty that is exceedingly rare in this business." **Ritch Esra – Former Executive at A&M Records and Arista Records. Currently, the Publisher of A&R Registry**

"Eugene Foley is the consummate professional. He's knowledgeable, experienced and well connected throughout the music business. For services such as career guidance, marketing, radio promotion, publicity and much more, he's the guy you want in your corner. He's quite simply a music industry genius. Period." **Steve Parry – Formerly signed to Columbia Records & currently a Product Information Specialist at Disc Makers**

"Eugene Foley comes with years of experience in career consulting, as well as helping you market and promote your CD. Basically, he helps you get a leg up and puts you on, (maybe not the fast track,) but the right track to helping your music succeed. And, he's a stand up guy. Always fun to talk with on the phone." **Alex Steininger – CD Baby Executive**

"Eugene is definitely a professional! He has a well-honed ability and proven background that relates to artists and their needs. He can offer valuable guidance and assistance for their overall growth, and success." **Don Grierson – Former A&R Executive at Epic, Capitol and EMI**

"Eugene Foley...A real honest pro in biz full of spineless, heartless, gutless chumps who make a ton of money doing nothing... Trust me, I've seen it all...Eugene is a rare breed of music industry people who care...WOW...CARE...What a concept...Everyone who even thinks about getting into the shark tank A/K/A "THE MUSIC BIZ" should learn one thing from Eugene — and that is to really care and love what you do." **Steve Brown – Formerly signed to MCA Records. Gold record winner**

"Eugene Foley is exactly the kind of upstanding and forthright person that I like to do business with. He is dependable and friendly at all times, and I look forward to our next opportunity to work together." **Jim Nelson – Music Industry Executive**